MADE
FOR
MORE

MADE
FOR
MORE

PHYSICIAN ENTREPRENEURS
WHO LIVE LIFE AND PRACTICE MEDICINE
ON THEIR OWN TERMS

COMPILED BY NNEKA UNACHUKWU, MD

Made for More

*Physician Entrepreneurs Who Live Life and
Practice Medicine on Their Own Terms*

ISBN 978-1-5445-3822-8 *Hardcover*
      978-1-5445-3820-4 *Paperback*
      978-1-5445-3821-1 *Ebook*
      978-1-5445-4007-8 *Audiobook*

To the students and alumni of the

EntreMD Business School.

Your courage to go after your dreams makes you

shining examples of what is possible.

You are the cavalry the physician community

has been waiting for.

CONTENTS

SECTION II

STARTUPS

SECTION III
THRIVING AS A PHYSICIAN ENTREPRENEUR

INTRODUCTION

I knew the results would be the same, but I tried again. I opened my laptop, pulled up my Chrome browser, and entered the words "physician entrepreneur" in the Google search bar.

And just like I expected, not much came up.

This was in 2010, when Facebook groups, coaching, podcasts, and YouTube channels were not as popular as they are now. I had just started my first business, a private practice, fifteen months after residency—and with two children under the age of two.

I wondered, *What's wrong with being a doctor, working a job, and being completely content with that? Why do I want more?*

I felt alone. I felt like a misfit. I even felt guilty.

What was wrong with me? Why would making six figures, working five days a week with no call not be enough?

I didn't know. What I did know was that there was more, and I wanted it. (I didn't even know what "it" was, but I wanted it.) So I started a private practice.

No one needed to tell me that starting a practice fifteen months after graduating from residency was not the smartest of ideas—I knew that! So why did I decide to go along with it anyway? Because I wanted more.

Once I started the practice, I realized that I was way out of my league. I was a physician, not an entrepreneur, and nothing in my medical training had prepared me to run a practice that would serve well and earn well.

If you're like me, you may be feeling like many things are working against you as you try to grow and scale your business, chief among them the fact that you don't have a business education. You may think you can't do this, but I hope this book will help you see that your fears are normal. As physicians, we have been told to stay in our lane, but you can *make your own lane*. Bad as these setbacks may seem, you can thrive.

I started my pediatric practice with the erroneous mindset that I could hang the proverbial shingle and people would come, but I learned very quickly that being a good doctor was not enough to grow a busy practice. I had to become a student again. I had to learn how to market my business as a professional, hire personnel, build a strong company culture, and understand the financials.

This was particularly tough because I had started my entrepreneurial journey as a super shy, socially awkward introvert. I had to learn to speak, network, and put myself out there confidently.

I learned primarily from books, the small circle of entrepreneurs that I had access to at the time, and good old trial and error. But although these things helped, what I really wanted was business ideas and stories from people like me. I would have given a lot to be in the same room with other physician entrepreneurs, asking them questions and learning from their stories, but they were nowhere to be found.

Well, that was twelve years ago. Since then, my practice has been very successful and thrived even in the middle of a pandemic. Despite this success, I kept exploring what "more" was for me. Even though I am an introvert, I created hundreds of videos, launched two podcasts, and hosted live events with as many as 500 doctors registered. I even founded the EntreMD Business School, a school designed to help doctors like me start profitable businesses so they can live life and practice medicine on their terms.

Now I've compiled stories from over forty doctors from the EntreMD Business School, who are sharing their own journeys as physician entrepreneurs. Some of these doctors are full-time employees building their brands, and others run private practices, coaching practices, nonprofits, and so forth. Some have just started out, some just hit their first $100K, and others are making multiple millions every year. But every one of them had fears, self-doubt, lack of experience, and many other things that could have stopped them. They just decided to dare them all and move forward.

And the best part is that for many of them, they have just begun. They are going to go on and shatter one glass ceiling after the another.

This book was written so that you don't have to Google the term "physician entrepreneur," so that you don't have to have the same experience as me. If you're wondering where other physician entrepreneurs are, they are all right here.

Their stories will inspire you, open up your eyes to new possibilities, and show you practical steps you can take. They will make you realize that wanting more is normal. Wanting to have a reach far outside the exam room is normal. Wanting to explore all your potential is normal.

And no matter what you've been told, you can do it!

—Dr. Una

UNLOCKING YOUR BUSINESS **IDEAS**

One of the most common things I hear from physicians who want to start businesses is that they don't have any business ideas.

The truth of the matter is that almost every physician is walking around with at least three very good business ideas. To uncover these ideas, you have to take inventory:

- What are the things you are good at?
- What challenges have you overcome?
- What are the things you would do even if no one paid you?
- What experiences, certifications, and expertise do you already have?
- What is a problem that always gets your attention?

You may take inventory and decide you only want to devote yourself to climbing the corporate ladder. Even if you want to do that, you have a business—your personal brand! You may not be a traditional employee but a special type of entrepreneur: an intrapreneur.

Throughout this section, you will read the stories of real-life doctors who have discovered their profitable business ideas. Many of them never thought of themselves as entrepreneurs, did not have any business education, and had all the fears that typically stop others. Through their stories, you will realize what is possible for you too.

CHAPTER 1

THE
PURPOSE-DRIVEN
PHYSICIAN

At age thirty-four, I had a picture-perfect family. By the grace of God, I was still married to my soul mate, and we were blessed with a very empathic five-year-old son and a delightful infant boy. But shortly before I finally completed my medical training, we almost lost everything.

I was holding our newborn at home while getting ready for bed when my husband suddenly ran into the room to announce smoke was coming out of the walls. There was a fire in our house, and we had to evacuate. I called 911 while getting dressed.

I held our newborn inside my long coat and put a hat on our older child before running outside into the bone-chilling darkness. We watched the fire truck and just waited. That night was the last time I saw our house and all our possessions inside. Everything burned down to the ground.

The period that followed was a whirlwind of intense ups and downs. I cried, and my family cried, but the experience gave me a new outlook on life. My family and I could have been burned to ashes along with our possessions, but that didn't happen. I realized that life is a gift; today is a gift; tomorrow is not guaranteed.

When I almost lost everything, what is most meaningful and worthy of pursuing became uncomfortably clear. The rest, including the professional expectations physicians work so hard to meet, was just noise. I realized I was truly responsible for how I live my life. Yet I was not quite ready for a complete transformation.

At the end of medical training, I was proud to wear an invisible survivor badge. I had survived having a newborn as an intern, despite regularly being away for thirty hours. I had survived countless step exams, in-training exams, and written and oral board exams, despite chronic sleep deprivation. I had survived a second pregnancy while in training. I had survived a house fire. I had survived, but I had lost a part of myself—I had lost my spirit.

Who was that young woman who had applied to medical school? She majored in astrophysics at a prestigious college. She traveled the world during her junior year abroad. In her travels, she connected with many people from different cultures and walks of life. She deeply believed these genuine interactions reflect what is most beautiful about being human. Back in the United States, she volunteered in an inner-city emergency room, where she was humbled to see patients in their most vulnerable moments, after car accidents and heart attacks. She was drawn to the intensity of this profession. She wanted to be there when patients needed lifesaving interventions, viewing that responsibility and ability to help as a privilege.

To that young woman, applying to medical school was applying to be a superhero. But I had forgotten her fierce passion and determination.

When I finally became an attending physician, I did not get a superhero cape; I got a computer login, an ID badge, and an RVU target. But I was grateful to make payments on my student loans, I enjoyed seeing patients, and life was more manageable. We welcomed our third child, and though I still spent many late nights completing work, I felt I had a good work environment. Finally, my family and I could settle down in a beautiful little town and grow roots.

Several years later, changes started happening at work. Then COVID-19 came, with yet more changes occurring. Doctors lost their jobs. Decisions were being made, without any discussion, that directly and indirectly affected my practice.

I could only watch; I felt powerless. I still had the heart to take care of patients, but my heart was weighed down by feeling devalued. I wasn't allowing myself to process all my feelings. I just felt the instinct to run away.

I thought of my options. I could search for another job, but I had believed I'd signed up for my ideal job, and my family would have to move again. Feeling further demoralized, I considered leaving medicine. Were other professionals feeling as discouraged as doctors? Perhaps I could find out.

I decided to sign up for my first non-medical conference, a life planning workshop for financial advisors. At that conference, I did something I had never done before—I volunteered to be "on stage."

This was not role-playing; I was getting actual life planning. The instructor asked me to share what mattered the most to me, and then he listened intently, empathetically, and without any judgment. For the first time, I was able to deeply and honestly reflect on what is important to me, to imagine who I want to be and what I want to do. Not just for tomorrow or next week, but my entire life.

Then the life planner vividly described a moment in the future filled with the elements that mattered the most to me. I felt my dream become reality. I was so touched that I started crying in front of twenty-five strangers. I didn't realize it at the time, but that was the moment I needed to spark my transformation.

I started to recognize the young woman applying to medical school who was full of optimism, courage, and strength. I started to value my dreams: to help people, to transform lives, to make an impact, and to honor each person's humanity—especially in their vulnerable moments. I wanted to leave a legacy in the world, through my professional work, loving my family, and raising my children.

I had applied to medical school to get a superhero cape, but my employment contract did not list that. I concluded there is nothing inherently wrong with my employed position; it just does not fully encompass the vision I have for myself.

To reach my vision, I discovered a new identity for myself: an entrepreneur. Previously, I had thought that "entrepreneur" was a dirty word, but I now say it with pride. An entrepreneur is one who wants to create the opportunity to serve and earn, because her dreams are so bold and cutting-edge that she simply cannot find a job description to match them.

Before, I was a reserved introvert who didn't want to bother people. Now I am fully responsible for my life and pursue goals that are aligned with my purpose. I am owning my voice and growing my audience.

I started my own business to help physicians find what is meaningful to them and design a life that gives them true fulfillment. I started a weekly podcast. I even chose to stay as a part-time employee at the same institution, where I am serving in leadership roles and bringing in physician wellness initiatives.

I celebrated when I got my first paying client, my first paid speaking gig, and my first note from a stranger raving about my podcast. I am full of hope for the future and proud of my cape waving in the wind.

Every physician can live a fulfilling, purpose-driven life. We don't have days to waste, because tomorrow is not guaranteed. We can choose to start living the life we want today.

Author: Dr. Weili Gray

Dr. Weili Gray loves building her dream life with her husband and three children in the Northeast Kingdom of Vermont. She practices sleep medicine and adores the patients she sees in her rural community.

She is passionate about helping doctors find their own dreams and start living them sooner than they imagined. As a Registered Life Planner and CEO of Dare to Dream Physician, she hosts an inspirational podcast by the same name, speaks at events, facilitates workshops, and works one-on-one with clients.

You can follow Dr. Gray on Instagram: @dreamphysician.

CHAPTER 2

JOURNEY OF A **RECOVERING** ACADEMIC

Thinking beyond Research Grants

The question of where I saw myself in five years always made me cringe. I honestly was just trying to keep my head above water, trying desperately not to drown. How would I even survive another six months, let alone another five years?

I had been going through the motions for about a year when I hit rock bottom. I had been promoted to associate professor with tenure, but it was twelve months of trying to hide my mental exhaustion, shame, and defeat. The road to promotion was grueling. I didn't think I could take more of the same to advance to full professor.

For over a decade, I had thrived in the academic environment. I began my academic career at a time when teaching future pediatricians how to counsel families about parenting was based on personal experience or what you heard your attending say, so I decided to adapt an evidence-based parenting program originally developed in psychology and translate it for pediatrics. My ideas soon became the seeds of research grants.

The expectation was to write and submit a grant each cycle. However, when grants don't materialize, one's time is covered by taking on more clinical time or administrative duties. As years went on, my days were filled with countless meetings that generated to-do lists, increasing clinical time and teaching. My time for writing grants was delegated to late nights and weekends.

In December 2018, I left my job in academia. I didn't have a plan; I just knew something had to change.

My entrepreneurial journey did not begin the moment I quit my academic job. It took time and patience, a willingness to be okay with uncertainty, and the love and support of my family and friends. It was eighteen months before I finally discovered I was not only a "recovering academic" but also a "budding entrepreneur." In the interim, I had started a part-time behavioral health private practice. That was a "safe zone" because so much of my identity was as a behavioral pediatrician seeing patients.

During the pandemic, the mental health needs of families with children with ADHD were amplified more than ever before. Children were now doing remote learning. Parents were thrust into the role of teacher and feared their children were falling behind. I thought, *What if I could help families and children through this time?*

I realized I could. Yet, this time there was no waiting for grant funding, consulting my mentors, or a formal peer-review process—it was both terrifying and invigorating.

The ideas started flowing. Within a few hours, I had produced an outline and flyer asking for family volunteers. Before I could back out, I posted the flyer on social media and waited.

Ten days later, I had six families, which was more than enough for a group program. Even though my idea had not been entirely fleshed out, families had volunteered. It was proof families needed what I could provide. The voice of my research mentor echoed: "Ideas are cheap, but implementation is where the 'rubber hits the road.'" I rolled up my sleeves and got to work.

The next two months were a blur. I had facilitated in-person groups before, but I planned for the program to be virtual due to the pandemic. Plus, my ideal clients were families. Therefore, the new program needed a fun and engaging theme.

That was how the All Deeds Help Detective Agency was born. Families would assume the roles of junior and senior detectives. I would broadcast from "headquarters" (HQ) and would create deeds for each "training mission meeting." I wove in positive parenting concepts into the family missions assigned in between sessions. Families would send in "evidence" to get feedback from HQ. I even developed a fun mission map for the detectives.

Participation for busy families needed to be easy, which is why I came up with the idea of putting class supplies in a box. I had a steady flow of Amazon boxes delivered as supplies were ordered. I developed and printed handouts in keeping with my detective theme, and then I repackaged everything.

I turned my focus to thinking through the logistics of the weekly meetings. As kids and parents were taking the class together, weekends or after school and work were best. So I picked a start date and sent Zoom links to the volunteers.

I quickly fell into a rhythm. I used the day after each class to make presentation adjustments based on family feedback and my own notes. Then I spent the rest of the week working on the following week's materials.

Before I knew it, eight weeks were done. Reading over testimonials I received from families, I realized that I had a proof of concept for what has now become my signature TEACH ME ADHD program.

Discovering that an idea is viable and can help families is rewarding. However, I would have never realized this if I had allowed the idea to stay in my head. Now, as an entrepreneur, I can test an idea quickly and realize immediate impact. This is what I had craved all along.

I view my academic past as stepping-stones to my present life. However, I have shed the crippling need to measure my worth by the size of grants or the number of peer-reviewed publications on my curriculum vitae.

As an entrepreneur, there is no "bar" other than what I set for myself.

I embrace the freedom entrepreneurship has given me. It is liberating to have control over my time and to choose which ideas become reality as CEO of my own business. In the process, I have found an outlet for my creativity and gained a renewed sense of purpose.

I now know I can never truly hit rock bottom; if I fall down, I only have to get up and take a step forward.

Author: Dr. Nerissa S. Bauer

Dr. Nerissa Bauer is a board-certified pediatrician who left academia due to burnout in December 2018. She now has a part-time behavioral pediatrics private practice, is the CEO of Let's Talk Kids Health, and is the creator of TEACH ME ADHD, her signature course for kids and parents to take together. She is also the host of *Let's Talk Kids Health LIVE* and a spokesperson for the American Academy of Pediatrics.

Dr. Bauer lives with her husband, two kids, and two goldens in Carmel, Indiana. Find out more about her on Instagram: @letstalkkidshealth.

CHAPTER 3

DELIVERING MD
VERSION 2.0

I sat with my head between my legs, blood pouring into the toilet bowl. I had delivered my third baby five weeks before, and the clots now came briskly from my uterus. As an OB/GYN, I was no stranger to blood—massive amounts of it. However, I was now terrified.

My husband and I rushed to the nearest emergency room. My blood pressure was low, my heart rate high, and I needed a blood transfusion. As I lay there on the gurney dizzy and tired, I thought to myself, *Wow, this is how my patients who bleed from their fibroids must feel.*

I started recounting the stories of so many patients—the bleeding and clots, iron and blood transfusions, visits to the emergency room, hospitalizations, the fatigue, emergency surgeries, loss of time from work and family, the financial burden of buying so many sanitary products, and the decreased quality of life. How did they do it month after month?

I had dreamed about starting my own practice when I finished medical school. A homey office, a wonderful staff, ample time with my patients, and flexibility in my schedule. My kids could even hang out with me in the office on days off or if they were sick. I would take enough vacations and make it to most plays and sports games. I didn't know my specialty yet, but I knew the type of lifestyle that I wanted.

Fast forward to 2021, and the reality of how I practiced medicine was very different. Minimal flexibility, loss of autonomy, not enough vacation, and definitely not enough control over my schedule to make most of my kids' events. My schedule was predetermined by high heels and clipboards that knew little about the actual art and science of medicine. I was a cog in a giant corporate wheel. My job security was even threatened by "providers" who had a fraction of my training and experience, unbeknownst to patients.

I realized if I wanted to create my ideal practice—the one I imagined for myself at the end of medical school—I had to develop a new mindset and skills. I had to become a newer version of myself, version 2.0.

So I made one of the best decisions of my life: to join the EntreMD Business School (EBS). The curriculum is unique, practical, and emphasizes action over information consumption. It has led me to rediscover my mission in life and my purpose in medicine. And doing it with a tribe of forward-thinking, like-minded physicians has been invigorating and motivating.

I have decided to use my training and advanced surgical skills to serve women with fibroids and abnormal bleeding. I want to help them to live a life free of bleeding and pain, to optimize their fertility, and to have an improved quality of life. What I experienced that one time was scary enough—no one should have to go through that on a regular basis.

To live out this mission, I realized that I had to do many things, the most important being "building my brand." Although corporate medicine "markets," I have no control over when, how, and to whom. Traditional marketing via radio, TV, and print is almost obsolete, and social media now leads the way. I grew up with sites like Friendster and MySpace, but the mediums today are much more complex and sophisticated. Even the way that patients obtain medical information and find doctors has changed.

Through encouragement from EBS, I have made great strides in establishing myself in the digital space. In July 2021, The Fibroid Doc was born, and I have started YouTube, TikTok, and Instagram channels to educate women on fibroids and abnormal bleeding. I have also learned how to conduct Facebook and Instagram lives, interact with online audiences, run a webinar, start a website, and collaborate with guests on podcasts. I have been consistent in putting out information weekly to attract my ideal clients.

Now, let me be clear, all of this didn't happen by magic. I had to make a commitment to change—and to embrace progress over perfection. I had to start becoming comfortable with being *uncomfortable*. I had to put myself out there in front of people I did not know. I had to ask for referrals, speaking opportunities, and network in a new way, landing myself in spaces with people who could help me further my mission. This was all in addition to my regular work as a full-time OB/GYN, wife, and mother to three small kids!

The process of transforming myself into a newer version requires laser focus. I have developed new habits. I have stopped wasting time on my phone, used social media strategically to get my message out, and read more in the last quarter than I did all of 2020. Even in my job as an employed physician, I have refocused, only handling revenue-generating activities such as seeing patients; I leverage my staff and my team to help me with all other tasks. Similarly, on the home front, I have outsourced many things so that I can enjoy quality time with my family and get seven hours of sleep every night!

Becoming version 2.0 has brought me closer to my dream of building my ideal practice. I am equipping myself with the skills I need to pivot, learn, and reshape my future. One day, I will leave corporate medicine to build my dream practice—and to live out my mission of serving women with fibroids and abnormal bleeding. This ongoing transformation has been possible because of EBS, the support, and the common mission that drives us: to practice medicine on our own terms.

Author: Dr. Cheruba Prabakar

Dr. Cheruba Prabakar is an OB/GYN and fellowship-trained mini-mally invasive surgeon. She is the founder and CEO of The Fibroid Doc and helps women with fibroids live a life with reduced bleed-ing, pain, and improved fertility. She has also been a speaker at the Essence Festival and has been a medical correspondent for Arise America.

Dr. Prabakar practices in the Bay Area and lives in Oakland, California with her husband, three kids, and two cats! You can follow her on Instagram: @thefibroiddoc.

CHAPTER 4

WHEN DREAMS CHANGE

Using Entrepreneurship to Expand Your Vision

"You see things; and you say, 'Why?' But I dream things
that never were; and I say, 'Why not?'"

—George Bernard Shaw

Have you ever wondered if there was *more* to you than being a doctor?

I didn't. Not at first.

Growing up, I had only two dreams: to become a neonatologist, a fellowship-trained pediatrician who takes care of premature and critically ill newborns, and to become the medical director of a neonatal intensive care unit (NICU) so I could improve the quality of neonatal care. Yet, through a series of life's changes and personal revelations, I realized I had a new dream: to be both a doctor *and* an entrepreneur. Becoming a physician entrepreneur would give me the freedom to practice medicine the way I envisioned, to spend quality time with my family, and to make a *huge* impact, leaving a legacy.

I conceived my business idea, developed a name and logo, registered the business as a limited liability company (LLC), filed for a tax ID number, created a lead magnet and landing page, and even worked with a few paid clients—in less than nine months! But this required a *massive* mindset shift. I was afraid to become an entrepreneur, and I held fast to my initial dreams because I believed I was giving up by desiring something different, wanting something more.

I've learned many lessons as a new entrepreneur, and I'm still learning! Here are two key lessons that I learned.

Lesson #1: It is *okay* for your dreams to change and for your vision to expand.

Changing your dreams and goals for your life does not mean you are giving up. It means you're evolving! And evolution is necessary for growth and success.

Are you holding on to an old dream, too afraid to *pivot*?

Here is my story; perhaps it is like your own.

I worked hard in school to become a doctor. I was so excited when I completed pediatrics residency training and was accepted into a neonatology fellowship, despite having my son at thirty-one weeks during my last year of residency.

But I finished only nine and a half months of fellowship; I resigned because I wasn't thriving. I was separated from my premature son and my husband, who could not relocate, so I rejoined my family and found the perfect job as a neonatal hospitalist in a level 2 NICU. I could still take care of sick newborns and help their families; I simply didn't have the title "neonatologist."

For a while, this was hard for me to accept. Individuals in medicine are typically driven and unwavering. We do not like detours! I was a failure in my mind, even though life's circumstances affected my dream. For five years, I struggled with the decision to return to the fellowship program. I now had kids and a good salary. I was still helping premature infants and their families and was even promoted to medical director, my other dream. Yet, I started to leave work, crying at times, because I needed a change.

I've always believed my work should be connected to my purpose. So I asked myself, *What do I like about my current job and what would I change? What do I really want for my life now, and how do I want to spend my time?* I knew I enjoyed taking care of babies and counseling, educating, and reassuring moms about their transition to motherhood. I also still enjoyed working in the NICU. But I wanted freedom from corporate medicine and to spend more time with my family.

The answer was clear: I had to become an entrepreneur. The more I visualized what my desired life could be, the more I recognized the power I had to make it happen.

You have the power too! You simply need to shift your thinking and understand the power of working for yourself, manifest the vision(s) inside of you, and uncover the reason for your pivot.

Lesson #2: To be an entrepreneur, you need the will to work for yourself and to own your why.

The *will* to be an entrepreneur was the hardest mindset shift for me. Working for myself would be too much work, and I was afraid to fail. My hospital patients constantly asked me to open my own practice, but I always said, "I simply want to go to work, take care of my patients, and go home." Sound familiar?

Working in the hospital meant I didn't have to worry about overhead, staffing, marketing, or securing patients. However, I became discouraged by corporate medicine and the politics involved. I learned that working as a physician is hard work, whether I work for others or for myself. But by working for myself, I could create the life I wanted and make changes in my company as necessary. I could still serve my ideal client and thrive financially.

I had a choice: develop the will to work for myself or stay with the status quo. I chose to work for myself and realized my why helped me with that—I wanted to spend quality time with my children, own my time, and carry out the visions inside of me.

You need your will and your why because the entrepreneurial journey is not without ups and downs. Your will and why will carry you through the emotional upheavals and setbacks that will come and the constant temptation to stay in your comfort zone. As an entrepreneur, you will fight fear, indecision, overwhelm, and doubt. But you will also experience the freedom and peace that comes with doing what you are meant to do.

If everything was done for you and you only had to show up

in your zone of genius, would you do it? If the answer is yes, then become an entrepreneur and bring that dream to fruition! It will be hard, but you can do hard things. How do I know? Because you already did! You are a doctor!

Take one step and then another, like I did. I have now done Facebook lives and been a guest on more than one podcast. I even joined the EntreMD Business School community to be supported by like-minded doctors and get a framework for how to succeed as a physician entrepreneur.

Do it scared! Embrace your vision, activate your will, own your why, and begin! The sky is the limit!

Author: Dr. Jessica Daigle

Dr. Jessica "Jess" Daigle is a board-certified pediatrician and NICU/pediatric hospitalist. She is a former NICU medical director at Wellstar Spalding and is currently the Founder/CEO of Mom & Me MD, a fourth trimester/postpartum care practice to help new moms and NICU moms transition home from the hospital.

Dr. Daigle has been featured on many podcasts, including *Pregnancy Pearls* with Dr. Plenty and *Defeat Postpartum Depression* with Arielle Wozniak. She is also a contributing writer for Verywell Health and has a YouTube channel titled Jess Daigle, MD.

She lives in Atlanta, Georgia with her husband and two kids. Follow her on Instagram: @momandme_md.

CHAPTER 5

UNSTOPPABLE
CONFIDENCE

I am a clinician, physician leader, and a C-suite executive. I am a teacher, mentor, sponsor, coach, and speaker. I've built teams and developed business strategies. I am a mom of two teenage boys and the firstborn daughter of elderly parents. All this adds up to a whole lot of experience and power wielded every day, but it only counts as power if you recognize it.

Early in my career, I was one of two physicians hired in leadership roles after residency. My initial salary offer was decreased in the final contract, and the reason given was that the other candidate, a man, "needed to make more money because he had a family," even though I had more qualifications. I didn't know how to fight back.

A few years later, an opportunity for promotion arose, and I was advised not to apply because I was not "sufficiently experienced," despite the fact that I had been second in command for more than five years. Events like these along the journey can be discouraging, and I didn't have the confidence to push back.

One day, I decided I'd had enough, and I was going to step into my courage. I declared my candidacy for the promotion and eventually got it. I decided then to build my confidence and step into my power.

You likely have areas in your life where you are directing multiple moving parts every day, yet professionally you hesitate to step up to a higher role or to launch a business. The first thing to realize is that you're *already* a boss.

It is not about your qualifications either. I should know—I have an MD, MPH, MBA, and a few additional fellowships and certifications. I am a lifelong learner, but also perhaps at the back of my mind I thought I needed these qualifications to prove I can do hard things, and that is just not true. The truth is, I have been a leader and a boss all along. By the time I earned my MBA, I had already proven that I could start a business or take a position of leadership. I had already done it. What I needed was confidence.

Let me share a few key points I've learned over the years in my journey.

Evolve your thinking: Stop thinking of yourself as *just* a clinician or *just* anything. You must get to a place where you can lead yourself and your team with confidence. You do that by owning your knowledge and expertise deliberately. Stop and think, *Do I have the required skills and resources to do this job and take the next step?* Imagine having this conversation with your sister who wants to start a business. You'd most likely say, "You've got this." Give yourself that same grace.

Distill your experience: All of your experience, good and bad, adds up to who you are, so distill it and bring it forward. Joseph

Campbell, author of *The Hero's Journey*, posits that life is not a straight path. It is winding, with dips and highs. Every time you go into a dip—such as illness, divorce, job loss, or other challenges—you emerge with a gift. The purpose of that gift is to take you to the next level. Every experience you have is designed to enrich you for the next phase of the journey. You've been through a bunch of dips, and you've learned a lot, so bring the gifts to your next platform.

Reflect and be still: Give yourself time to be silent and reflect. Think about what you want to do and what tools you need. When you're running on autopilot, you only access the things that are built into autopilot and not your full range of skills and resources. Take time to reflect and be still, to think, focus, and get clarity. Journaling or a meditation practice can be invaluable in this quest.

Own your expertise: Don't apologize or explain it. You've worked hard to get where you are. Address the imposter syndrome that makes you question your qualifications. Think about how mad you'd be if somebody who is clearly less qualified than you are does—with apparent ease—what you're hesitant to do. Let that motivate you. Recognize that your passion or idea is a gift that you have a responsibility to share. Then you'll have urgency to share and not hold it to yourself. It gives you the impetus and the energy to keep going forward.

Humble brag: You may think "my work speaks for me," but work does not speak. All it does is generate more work. You must speak. Practice the "humble brag." When you do something, say you did it, even if you say it to only yourself. Marking the accomplishment helps you to own it. Share your wins and stories via newsletters, periodic updates to your team and stakeholders, speaking engagements, videos, even social media. Cataloging your skills and accomplishments empowers you to step forward confidently. You've done the work; nobody is doing you a favor. You are bringing your gift forward, bought and paid for with your blood, sweat, and tears.

When I left my employer after a decade, there was such a reaction in the community that the CEO called and asked me to please make a statement indicating that I was leaving of my own accord and not because of anything they had done. What a difference confidence makes!

I hope I can convince you to step into your confident self. Remind yourself of all that you have accomplished and the impact you have had. It wasn't easy or benign; you did hard things, and you need to recognize it so others can recognize it too. I want you to change your life and, in the next ninety days, to say, "I did not know I could be *this* unstoppable."

Author: Dr. Nwando Anyaoku

Dr. Nwando Anyaoku, aka Dr. A, is VP and Chief Health Equity Officer for Swedish Health Services in Seattle. A board-certified pediatrician, professor, and experienced physician executive, Dr. A is an inspiring speaker with multiple media, conference, and podcast appearances on topics including leadership and health equity. She is also a coach for physicians seeking to thrive in healthcare organizations, as well as the founder of Omugobaby, a digital platform that connects parents of newborns to doula services.

Dr. A lives in Seattle, Washington with her two sons, her why. You can find her on LinkedIn: @nwandoanyaoku.

CHAPTER 6

CREATING
ABUNDANCE

" **H** e holds on to your dress and screams whenever anyone tries to take it from him," my husband said again. The "he" my husband was referring to was my nine-month-old son. My husband explained that our son would hold on to my clothing during the day while I was at work.

For the first time in my life, working harder did not create more. Working harder did not create more time, more security, or more peace. My son was clinging to my clothing while I was working— I knew something needed to change.

How can I create more without losing more time with my family? What skills do I possess? My only passion was helping people lose weight and reverse disease, but I was too afraid to say it aloud because I feared no one would understand my outrageous ideas or someone would reply, "Oh, everyone is doing that."

I started my attending career practicing pain management in an inner city, but I found myself more of an interrogator than a doctor. I would spend hours reviewing potential patient charts, drug monitoring systems, urine toxicology police reports for lost/stolen medication, and discharge letters to ensure the medication was being used for its intended purpose.

A disconnect is created when your days are filled with drug testing and half truths. There is a dread that overcomes you as you pull into the parking lot. There is a heaviness in your steps as you walk into work. I wondered, *How can I help people heal?*

I thought if I could help people lose weight, we could alleviate so many issues, so I studied obesity medicine and worked with hundreds of patients in an obesity medicine clinic. I traveled, visiting clinics to learn about reversing disease, water fasting, and farm-based healthcare systems. And for almost a decade, I secretly envisioned a healthcare program that would make people well again.

Even though I knew I wanted to help obese people, I was too fearful of own my vision. So when the opportunity to work at an occupational clinic arose, I pushed my scary dreams aside and accepted the position. This worked perfectly since no one knew of my secret vision…Until one day, I saw a firefighter who needed my secret information.

He was in his late thirties and only saw a doctor for his annual work physical. At that visit, he found out he was hypertensive and diabetic. He was placed on limited duty because his hemoglobin A1C was elevated. He wanted to know what he could do to turn back the clock, and I told him—on the condition that he obtain a primary care physician.

That firefighter did everything he was asked to do. In four weeks, he dropped his hemoglobin A1C by a percentage point. His blood pressure returned to normal range, he lost eight pounds, and he returned to full duty. Fascinating as these results were, it was nothing compared to the fact that he learned habits he used to maintain a healthier lifestyle. And after learning most first responders do not enjoy five years of retirement, I could not keep my vision secret any longer.

I joined EntreMD, where Dr. Una hammered in *"own it."* She said, "Your business can't be the best kept secret," so I started telling every patient who could benefit.

I then told my supervisors about my vision, giving presentations and asking to create a small program to focus on high-risk employees. My supervisors said yes and started funneling patients with uncontrolled diabetes to the program. Soon, I was able to help seven first responders decrease their hemoglobin A1C and return to work.

I created videos about simple health changes and sent them to patients, who responded that the videos helped them try new recipes and understand how to read food labels. I then created a YouTube channel using the video content. After hearing the same concerns repeatedly, I even started a podcast to help answer those questions. I sought out top experts in different fields, and to my surprise, they were willing to be interviewed! My first big ask was an accomplished PhD in chronological biology and TEDx speaker, and I was beyond excited to share the podcast and tips with every first responder I met.

Once, a firefighter provided lunch to the occupational clinic to introduce us to his nonprofit organization, which was created to help firefighters eat healthier while working in the fire station. He explained heart attacks were the number one cause of death of firefighters in the line of duty, and he believed the food served at the firehouse was one risk factor that could be modified. I invited him on the podcast, and we realized we shared a common goal. I was even asked to join the board of directors for that organization.

Then I finally stepped out and created my workplace wellness company, More Food Less Medicine. Every day, I am excited to pull into the parking lot, wondering, *Who will I help today?* There is a bounce in my step, and I am ecstatic to see data that reflects the changes in patients' improvement.

Despite adding all these things, I feel more aligned. Instead of taking extra shifts or working more hours, I am investing my valuable time in my vision. I spend more time with my family, and my son happily waves "bye-bye" because he knows he will see me and daylight at the same time now.

Along this journey I have learned three big lessons. First, creating something I am excited to share with others brings me joy and motivates me. Second, my ideas thrive in the midst of people who are dreamers like me. Third, own your unique dream.

Don't let your vision be a secret—your world is waiting for you.

Author: Dr. Michele Johnson

Dr. Michele Johnson is a fellowship-trained interventional spine and pain management specialist who holds board certifications in physical medicine and rehabilitation, pain management, obesity medicine, and lifestyle medicine. She is the founder of More Food Less Medicine, where she helps people with chronic diseases, such as type 2 diabetes mellitus, eliminate or decrease medications with simple foods. She is also the host of the *ZOEMD* podcast, a board member for the nonprofit organization Food on the Stove, and has been quoted in *Forbes* magazine.

Dr. Johnson resides in Washington, DC, with her husband and two children. You can follow her on Instagram: @drmichele johnson.

CHAPTER 7

CONNECTING WITH YOUR **WHY**

Ten years ago, I was surprised to find myself on the receiving end of charity. My son was born eight weeks early during what was supposed to be a three-day trip out of state. When I was released from the hospital, terrified and unprepared, my son was still in the NICU and would be there for at least another five weeks.

I got a room in the Ronald McDonald House across the street from the hospital, while my husband and daughter stayed with his family across town. The Ronald McDonald House had everything I needed: a comfortable room that a family had decorated, so it felt cozy, a closet full of tiny toiletry bottles that people had donated, and a pantry full of free food that I could take whenever I needed. They even had a playroom full of toys that my daughter loved so we could have a place to play when she visited. Because I could stay there, I was able to spend much more time in the NICU, including going several times overnight to hold my tiny baby. It was at the

Ronald McDonald House that I felt the power of small acts of giving, as I healed and leaned on those around me.

Over the years since then, I have been happy to give back, knowing what it's like to have that support when you need it. I have also been galvanized by the endless situations in the world where others do not have any support at all. I have learned more about those acts of giving, both big and small.

During the pandemic, at a time of personal struggle and much introspection, I decided I wanted to do more to help others be impactful in their giving. I had learned so much on my own giving journey, and I wanted to share that knowledge by starting a business to help physicians become effective philanthropists.

But that would mean putting myself out there in the world. I don't like to be uncomfortable, and what makes me really uncomfortable is doing anything that draws attention to myself. Being an introvert works fine for a radiologist but can be a real challenge if you want to be an entrepreneur—entrepreneurs need to put themselves out there. They need to live outside their comfort zones.

So I thought, *Maybe I shouldn't be doing this. I'm not one of those shiny people talking confidently on stage. Maybe I should give up.* I already had a career and a full life. Why did I keep pushing and dreaming? I could quietly walk away, and no one would know.

I almost did that so many times, but what kept me moving forward were two things: a mindset shift and finding my people.

My mindset shift actually came in a dream—I was in a gorgeous hotel in Paris. I had saved up my money for years to take a vacation in France and was at the end of the trip, getting ready to go to the airport and fly home. Then I realized I had never left the hotel during the entire trip. I hadn't gone out to a café to eat those amazing croissants. Why? Because I was afraid—afraid to make a fool of myself in French or be mocked as a ridiculous American tourist. I hadn't gone to the Louvre either. Why? Because I was confused— I didn't know how to find it, how to use the public transportation, and again was afraid to ask. So I missed out on it all. The walks on the streets, the food, the art. I was controlled by my fear. And I was so limited because of it.

When I woke up with that feeling of disappointment, I realized it would have been worth risking a little embarrassment to go to the café. It would have been worth it to work a little harder to figure out how to get to the museum. And I realized it would be totally worth it to be very uncomfortable in order to do this work that was truly meaningful and important.

With that mindset, I was ready to move forward with a business in which I could share my knowledge and help amplify the contributions we can all make together. I founded The Physician Philanthropist and developed a course for physicians to learn how to empower themselves with their giving, and how to develop effective philanthropy plans with the greatest personal, community, and worldwide impact.

Sometimes I still felt like walking away, but at those times, I was fortunate enough to have found my people: other physician entrepreneurs. With them, I felt safe and understood. I was supported, both practically and emotionally. Their constant encouragement and inspiration kept me going all those times I thought I would give up, and I kept moving forward.

It has been amazing to see that spark in people's eyes when we talk about giving and philanthropy, that moment when they realize they have power and can make a difference, even if they don't have billions of dollars to donate. People are now reaching out to me with their philanthropy questions and with collaboration opportunities. I have been interviewed on multiple podcasts by people I greatly admire, which was way outside my comfort zone and so worth it. I never gave up. I keep moving forward.

I truly believe that together we can do so much good!

Author: Dr. Recha Bergstrom

Dr. Recha Bergstrom is a women's imaging radiologist and the founder and CEO of The Physician Philanthropist, a company focused on helping doctors learn how to donate effectively and invest responsibly so that they can maximize their positive impact in the world. She also established The Physician Philanthropy Impact Fund, which takes the goal of healing and alleviating suffering in all its forms, globally, for people and the planet. Finally, Dr. Bergstrom writes the *Intentional Money* blog and has been a guest on several podcasts.

She lives in Northern California with her husband and three kids. Follow her on Instagram: @physicianphilanthropist.

CHAPTER 8

EMBRACE YOUR
FEARS!

The light at the end of the tunnel seemed more like an oncoming train than freedom. I had worked so hard and sacrificed so much throughout college, medical school, and residency with missed family get-togethers, holidays, and vacations. I would see my friends living their best lives and thought it would be all worth it once I started working as a physician. I thought I would finally be free when I finished training—I could go to lunch with my friends, travel the world when I wanted to, and never miss a family vacation or holiday again. But I was totally wrong.

The hours to get my practice up and running were longer than the eighty-hour workweek in residency. There was so much financial pressure to see more and more patients, and I struggled to keep up with all the paperwork. Every day, I felt overwhelmed and defeated. I had spent decades trying to get to this point in my life just to feel like I was in a prison.

I was so anxious about going to work every day that I would wake up several times during the night thinking about what would go wrong the next day. My anxiety turned to anger and resentment as I felt like I was losing control. My family and my patients noticed that I was not happy. Unfortunately, walking away from medicine was starting to look like an option. It just did not seem worth all the stress and anxiety to jeopardize my health or my family.

My mindset changed when I realized that seeing more and more patients in a fifteen-minute office visit wasn't what was going to make me happy, even though I had spent what felt like my entire life to get to that point. I realized there had to be a better way, a way I could help people improve their health without feeling so burned out that I wanted to quit altogether.

That is when I learned about business coaching and started working on a project where I could help more people outside the exam room. I set the foundation by registering my business, as well as hiring website developers and a branding specialist, thinking these were the most important steps. Soon, I had everything set, but I was not making any money. I realized I didn't know how to market my business to make it successful.

Then I attended a conference for physician entrepreneurs, where I heard Dr. Una speak about her business school. *This is what I was missing*, I thought.

I had sticker shock when I saw the price to join, though. I had already spent lots of money to get to this point in my business with nothing to show for all the work I had done. I wondered, *Will I just be wasting more money?* But the more pain, frustration, and anxiety I experienced every day, the more I knew something had to change. I decided to dedicate a year to the business school and go *all* in. So I signed up and was ready to go.

Then I was hit with what felt like a ton of bricks when the first assignment was to develop a signature talk. I felt defeated before even starting. I hate talking not just in front of a crowd but even in small circles. Growing up, I was so afraid of talking that I would be scared to call my grandmother and ask to go to her house, even though she would always say yes. Crazy, right? I wanted to skip this assignment, but I had already made the commitment and the yearlong investment into the business school.

We were given a speaking framework to follow, so I started recording videos and putting them on my YouTube channel. I didn't even know if anyone would watch the videos, but to my surprise, not only did people watch the videos; they told me they learned a lot from them. *It is actually working*, I thought. *Now I am getting clients from my YouTube channel.*

Next, I started asking people to be a guest on their podcasts. Once again, I was nervous to talk to someone live and have them ask me questions. My mind was flooded with doubt. *What if I don't know the answers? Am I going to look like a fool? I may lose business instead of gain business.* I had all this negative talk in my head, but my commitment to the business school kept pushing me forward.

After my first podcast, I felt relieved because I *did* know the answers, and I didn't look like a fool. It was actually fun. The more podcasts I did, the more I trusted my speaking. From all the speaking I was doing, I got more followers on social media and more on YouTube.

The ultimate test of speaking was to present to a live virtual audience. I was the keynote speaker for a conference, and though more fear and self-doubt tried to creep in, my previous success gave me confidence. I even got a paying client from the event. I have since been invited to be a guest speaker for a summit!

So in less than six months in EBS, I went from being terrified to talk to embracing the fear and doing it anyway. I am still nervous when I commit to doing any type of speaking, but I remove my selfish fears and keep my clients and my business mission in mind.

Learning to speak has dramatically changed my confidence and even helped my business make money. Initially, I started this business thinking it would be a little side hustle, but now I believe it is going to be bigger than I ever imagined!

Author: Dr. Amanda C. Adkins

Dr. Amanda Adkins is a board-certified internal medicine physician in Fairfield, California. She is the founder and CEO of Enlightenment Health and Wealth, where she helps women who are overweight prevent and/or reverse chronic diseases. She has been on several podcasts and served as a guest speaker and panelist discussing chronic disease in the Black community.

Dr. Adkins currently resides in the San Francisco Bay Area with her husband and daughter. Follow her on Instagram: @DrAmanda Adkins. On YouTube, search: Dr. Amanda Adkins.

CHAPTER 9

IGNITING THE FIRE WITHIN

"Ignite the fire within you, and it will allow you to
live your special dreams in life. You were born
for it and your destiny. Now...live it!"

—Timothy Pina

F ire can keep you warm, or it can burn you. It can be a source
of light, and it can also be a source of destruction. Fire is both
loved and feared, just like entrepreneurship. We fear what we do
not know—I know I did.

I am an emergency medicine (EM) doctor who had been practicing for over ten years but still felt a void in my life. I wanted
more, and I was fascinated by others who launched businesses,
but I wondered if I was being ungrateful. Why? Because as an EM
doctor, I thought my job was always secure. People would always
have emergencies and need my services. As the years passed, I
had thoughts about starting a business, but I extinguished them

because of fear. I was standing still while the world around me was changing. A pandemic was on the horizon, and little did I know that my world would change forever.

When the pandemic hit, my peers and I received notifications about pay cuts. Some of my colleagues even lost their jobs. I was shocked that doctors were fired during a global pandemic. What if I was next? I looked in the mirror and knew that I needed to take action. That day, I decided to work on overcoming my fears. So I began reading books on entrepreneurship, and I joined a group of physicians who, like me, wanted to start businesses.

I realized I could choose to be paralyzed by fear or use my situation as fuel to light the fire within me. I chose the latter, and in the fall of 2020, I launched UR Caring Docs, a telemedicine business.

The next step was, *how do I promote my business?* With an enormous push from a great mentor, I began making educational videos for social media. Every week for almost one year straight, I worked my regular EM job, then on my days off, made educational videos and streamed them live. Some days, I had ten people watching live, and other times, it seemed I was talking to an empty room. But I kept at it.

Little did I know, people were paying attention. One day, a woman sent me a message to tell me that her father was dying because of congestive heart failure, and she watched my videos every week because they were so helpful. I was humbled because I thought no one was listening, but I had made a difference. On one of the darkest days of this woman's life, she took the time to thank me. That was additional fuel.

After a few months, I realized I could not operate the telemedicine schedule and work full time. At first, I was embarrassed. I told the world I was starting a telemedicine business, but now I wanted to pivot. What would people think? Luckily I was surrounded by my tribe of entrepreneurs, who helped me work on my mindset. When I closed the business, I did not feel like a failure because course correction was part of the process.

I then focused on podcasting, doing a weekly live show with physician guests called Docs Who Care. The premise was simple: I wanted the world to see other doctors who care. I interviewed over one hundred doctors in four months! My audience started to grow, and I now have a waitlist of physicians who have signed up for interviews.

This journey made me realize that my fear was linked to my ego. We all have stories to share that will have a significant impact on others. With that in mind, I organized a female cancer awareness virtual mini-summit. Why not? I realized the effect would be greater than my fear. In just five weeks, three hundred people signed up from five different countries. The summit was a success, and the attendees are still sending positive reviews months later.

I then launched the UR Caring Society, a coaching program featuring expert speakers that helps busy professional women put their health and wellness first. This program will be my focus for the near future.

Starting any new project is hard and will initially be stressful. But the unknown can bring so much joy if you overcome fear and decide to start. When you have that fire within, fuel it with the right questions. Move from "I can't" to "How can I?" This shift will require daily practice, but it becomes easier with a bit of work.

It also helps to remind yourself that you can do hard things. Three months ago, I never thought I could organize a successful virtual mini-summit. But I did it because of my burning desire to help others.

You might be wondering, where do I stand now? Over the past year, I put my fear aside, surrounded myself with positivity, and got back up when I stumbled. I did it, *scared*. At times I wondered, *What in the world did I just do?* Then I looked around and said, "I became an entrepreneur!" Yes, that is what I did.

Author: Dr. Tamara Beckford

Dr. Tamara Beckford is an emergency physician living in Houston, Texas. She is the CEO of UR Caring Docs and the UR Caring Society, where she helps busy professional women put health and wellness first without guilt. Dr. Beckford also hosts the *Dr. Tamara Beckford Show*, where she has interviewed over 150 doctors about self-care, wellness, and the fantastic things they do outside of medicine.

When she is not speaking about self-care at conferences, she spends time with her husband and two young sons. Follow Dr. Beckford on LinkedIn: @drtamarabeckford.

CHAPTER 10

EMBRACE
DISCOMFORT TO
ELEVATE YOUR
DREAMS

W hen it became clear that I was on the brink of divorce, my
first thought was, *Oh boy, now I'll have to date again.* When
I share that with people, they usually think I am joking, but that's
my truth. Even during one of the most devastating moments of my
life, my biggest fear was discomfort.

Life is a series of uncomfortable moments. Medical school and
marriage definitely had their fair share. However, during my mar-
ital separation, I was actually coasting in my career. I had built up
a large patient panel and had a steady stream of patients to maintain a busy schedule. I had perfected the art of getting in and out
of the room (mostly) on time. My patients became so confident in
my timeliness that they would schedule to see me within thirty to

forty-five minutes of needing to be elsewhere in town. It was super hectic, but it was my normal, and I was comfortable.

However, that comfort came with a price. I was physically present, yet mentally absent, at home. I remember many days when my son would snuggle up to me while watching TV, because I had nothing left to give. (Kids always meet you where you are.) I had an early morning routine to an extent but no self-care regimen.

As a divorced mom with student loans and other obligations, I saw no way out. I thought about leaving the practice, but I dreaded leaving behind all the patients who had entrusted me with their care. And entrepreneurship was absolutely out of the question!

You see, I thought medicine was the dream. I had announced to my family that I would be a doctor at the age of four, when I only associated doctors with getting shots. But over time, I discovered that I had deferred many other dreams to pursue medicine. I realize now that medicine was the foundation and introduction to my future, but it was never meant to be the finish line.

Oddly enough, my eventual epiphany came through a quest for a "better body." By my mid-thirties, I had developed back and joint pain, acid reflux, heart palpitations, and anxiety. I limped and hobbled out of bed every morning. I was relying on caffeine for energy and was sugar-addicted. I was cycling and running but not putting the proper fuel into my body. I had prediabetes and elevated blood pressure, but I just thought that was part of the aging process.

It was through discomfort with my mirror image that I was startled into action.

To even consider dating, I knew I would need to feel better in my skin, so I pursued a new approach to weight loss. I found the lifestyle that suited me and started to change in a multitude of ways. Most importantly, I discovered the importance of wellness—optimizing my mind, body, and spirit in the process.

I knew early on that I needed to share this transformation with the world, and to do this justice, I would have to change my scenery. Leaving conventional medicine would certainly be uncomfortable. As an introvert, talking to strangers (a.k.a networking) was not my strong suit, and I wondered, *How would I make money? Would I lose my skills?* The only way I could envision practicing medicine was exactly the way I had already. To me, the people who left traditional medical practices were brave, and I was not brave!

And then the pandemic hit. Everything stopped, and we were forced to take a worldwide timeout. For me, this was a blessing, because I rediscovered things I had laid down long ago. I also started to see all these amazing physicians stepping out and doing unthinkable things!

I was led to start a podcast and unexpectedly loved the whole process—I officially had my own platform! But mindset is everything, and I still considered podcasting my hobby. It wasn't until I joined one of Dr. Una's virtual events that I was convinced I could be an entrepreneur. Yet, I was overwhelmed at the idea of starting, because trying something new would certainly bring discomfort. Needless to say, it took me a full seven months to push through my hesitations and invest in coaching. My limiting beliefs and their partners, despair and denial, had held me back for too long.

I decided to step fully into the discomfort and defined these limiting beliefs. There were ninety-three of them! I debunked and destroyed them (three per day for thirty-one days) as a gift to myself, and then I was finally able to see the tremendous head space these thoughts were taking up rent-free. They were cluttering my genius! I could now see clearly that my medical degree provided a path for my dreams, but I was free to take the route of my choice. For the first time in many years, I had a sense of purpose and the clarity of mind to pursue it.

The next few months were a whirlwind! I landed a new job that aligned with my passion, allowed me to work virtually, and provided me the flexibility to pick up my son from school each day. Not even six months later, I was featured in a magazine and launched my own wellness coaching program. Soon thereafter, I was asked to speak at three separate events planned for the following year! None of this was easy but was made possible through the meaningful, organic connections I made when I showed up as myself for myself. It was no longer an option to let my dreams go unlived.

Ultimately, had I kept adhering to my limiting beliefs, I would have continued worrying about things that would never come to pass. And surely, the discomfort I had worked so hard to avoid would have ensued anyway.

I have learned that limiting beliefs become limited dreams, which become wasted opportunities. Maybe you won't have to leap like I did, but you must not defer your dreams. They should come along with you every step of the way.

Now for this dating thing…

Author: Dr. Kamilah M. Williams

Dr. Kamilah M. Williams, also known as Dr. Milah, is double board-certified in family medicine and obesity medicine. She is the CEO of Pivot & Bloom and the creator and host of *The Single Well with Dr. Milah* podcast, where she empowers single moms to embrace wellness so that they can live full, illustrious lives. She was awarded the HEAL (Health Equity Achieved Through Lifestyle Medicine) Scholarship by the American College of Lifestyle Medicine to further her endeavor to improve healthcare disparities in her community through education.

Dr. Milah currently resides near Columbus, Ohio with her son. You can follow her on Instagram: @thechristianwellnessdoc.

CHAPTER 11

CONFIDENCE AND PERSONAL **GROWTH**

My name is Dr. Judit Andrea Staneata, and I am an intrapreneur! I work at an orthopedics and sports medicine clinic, but I also work for Dr. Judit Andrea Staneata, Incorporated, my personal brand. Despite my accomplishments, my narrative wasn't always so straightforward!

Upon the completion of my graduate medical training, I was excited to begin my first full-time position as a fully credentialed physiatrist with an interventional spine fellowship. Like many, I had preconceived notions of what my work-life balance would look like and had high expectations of my ability to manage it all.

The reality of my new situation sank in pretty soon, as well as the heaviness of my "golden handcuffs." My passion for healthcare is what drove me to this career in the first place, but despite my drive to provide exceptional care for my patients, I had scarce control over when I saw my patients, how they were treated, and my patient load!

As months and years passed by, I felt the joy of my responsibilities diminish, and my frustration gradually grew. I was trapped in a vicious cycle of trying to balance my professional obligations toward my patients with my personal obligations toward my family. As a single mother raising two young children, it was unnerving to know that I could not risk even temporary unemployment to change jobs. Knowing that there might be other, more advantageous facilities with open positions was encouraging at first. I began to explore my options, but the more I searched, the more one thing became abundantly evident: productivity was the foremost priority.

I chose to accept my suboptimal circumstances, but I always knew there had to be more to life. At one point, the opportunity arose to work in a different city. I thought to myself that this was the moment I had been waiting for! I had landed my dream job, after all. It was at a much bigger practice and appeared to appease my other preferences.

Unfortunately, this turned out to be a mirage. After I uprooted my children and myself to this new city, I was told that the new clinic would not honor my previously signed contract. This information was unexpectedly communicated to me just days before I was scheduled to start working there. I had never felt so lost in my entire life! I trusted this professional organization when I signed the contract and could not believe this could happen among fellow physicians. I kept telling myself that we were all colleagues. We were in this together with the ultimate objective of serving and helping people. In reality, I was just another number, and at that time, my position there did not line up with their corporation's needs.

I felt discouraged and scared and experienced a tremendous amount of shame, professionally and personally. I was already struggling with burnout on top of lifelong self-esteem issues of inadequacy. It seemed as though I wasn't doing enough, nor was I living up to others' expectations of me. The shame and sense of failure that I experienced was unparalleled. Thankfully, I was able to return to my old position on a part-time basis. It was around that time that I heard about coaching and started exploring options to rehabilitate and reframe my mindset.

As I was trying to figure out my next career steps, the coronavirus pandemic hit, and by the end of March 2020, I was furloughed. This was yet another devastating setback professionally and personally. I saw one of Dr. Una's ads about her podcast and began listening. Her words of encouragement and authenticity helped me through difficult times and improved my outlook on life. I finally realized I wasn't alone and could reach out for the help I needed. Prior to coaching, I struggled to put one foot in front of the other on a daily basis. I will forever be thankful to Dr. Una for offering her course at that time. I signed up, and the rest is history!

One of the most important things Dr. Una spoke of that resonated with me was that no matter my employment status, I work for myself! Dr. Una encouraged us to build our own brand, saying that every one of us has a story and a name, and that was our business. *Business?* I asked myself. I never in my life had thought about building a brand or business based on myself. I thought I was forever trapped in the eight-to-five cycle.

My mindset shift started. I finally began to see that it didn't have to be that way. As time progressed, I was able to secure a position with another employer, and from day one, I showed up with confidence and purpose. I realized that there is no perfect job, but we have the power to make the best of any situation.

At my six-month review, my employer asked me how they could help me to be more efficient and successful in my role. Knowing my capabilities and the inflow-outflow of patients, I immediately requested a scribe. My request was granted, and for the first time in my career, I not only was able to see more patients who needed help, but I also had more time with my children and for myself! I was finally able to breathe freely and not carry the weight of unfinished charts from day to day and week to week. I no longer spent twenty-plus hours over the weekends finishing notes from previous office visits. More importantly, I finally felt heard and valued!

As my mindset changed, I gained clarity, insight, and understanding. Since then, I have been saying yes and showing up for all kinds of opportunities! I signed up for the EntreMD Business School (EBS), and it has been life-changing both personally and professionally. Although I technically do not have my own business, I am building my brand as I continue to learn and grow. No matter how fast or slow I go, I will keep moving forward and say yes to future opportunities.

I continue to experience imposter syndrome, and I do get overwhelmed at times, but at EBS, I have learned that despite my fear,

I can overcome any obstacle. Because of this encouragement, I will continue to persist and achieve my goals. Our community is invaluable, and I know that I can rely on Dr. Una and my peers no matter what roadblocks I encounter on my journey.

Recently, I coauthored a bestselling book, in addition to being the guest on several podcasts, live webinars, TV, radio shows, and panel discussions. I went from experiencing extreme panic when creating my first video assignment to telling my life story in front of large audiences on both the national and international level! I will continue to become a better version of myself each and every day, and I am excited to see what the future has in store for me.

Author: Dr. Judit Andrea Staneata

Dr. Judit Andrea Staneata is board-certified in physical medicine and rehabilitation, fellowship-trained in interventional spinal procedures, and specializes in the nonsurgical treatment of conditions and injuries of the spine and musculoskeletal medicine. She is currently in practice with Cape Fear Orthopedics & Sports Medicine, providing services throughout the areas surrounding Fayetteville and Fort Bragg, North Carolina. She also coauthored an anthology called *The Warrior Women Project: A Sisterhood of Immigrant Women*, where she talks about her immigration story and her personal life experiences.

Dr. Staneata is passionate about empowering women to live their authentic lives despite difficulties and challenges. She lives in Spring Lake, North Carolina with her two children. Find her on Facebook as Andrea Staneata.

CHAPTER 12

THE **CAVALRY** IS ON THE WAY

The story you are about to read is the most public writing in my life to date. Not because I have become more confident in myself or what I have learned, but because physicians right now face an existential challenge too large to ignore. My story is one shared by most medical colleagues I know—a story whose next chapter we are already writing together.

I had what I would consider a typical experience with medical training: one of excitement, difficulty, and honor. Where this story begins, though, is with the moment I had no choice but to awaken from the disillusioned state I had been lulled into by corporate medicine.

I was enjoying my work in a small private practice when the owner decided to sell to a large hospital system in town. During the transition, I had to ask several times before they revealed the terms of their noncompete, which would have required that I move out of the city to be able to work if I ever left their system. That was the

73

first deal breaker. Even more, there was an intellectual property clause that gave them ownership over anything I did, even outside of their employed time. Since I already had part ownership of an addiction recovery program that my husband and I had created, this was the second deal breaker.

More saddening than an unworkable, non-negotiable contract was that when I asked my colleagues why they signed the contract, their answer was that they had to. That was the moment I felt what medicine has become. As physicians, we have been held hostage to our dedication to patients and doing what we know to be right. I knew that I needed to be a part of an evolved solution that stands not just for patients but also for physician livelihood.

During my unforeseen time off between this job and the next, I seriously considered my options. I contemplated lobbying as a physician advocate, building courses to empower physicians to negotiate, or even fleeing the situation entirely and staying at home with the kids. The upsetting thought was that I had spent so many years studying to be a physician, yet there I was without what I felt like were transferable skills, trapped without any choice but to keep my head down and reenter the new corporate version of medicine.

As serendipity would have it, I answered a recruiter's message on LinkedIn to work for an up-and-coming employee wellness company that provided onsite full primary care to large companies. I loved working there so much that I recruited several physicians to join me. Word spread, and friends started asking me to do the same for their private practices. I spent days on each placement, and I felt such satisfaction placing each doctor in a private practice where they felt happy again. It was like I saved them.

The reward from those favors evolved into the idea that I could really make an impact if I could do the same thing at a greater scale. I saw my friends' lives improve with their regained autonomy and could only imagine the downstream burdens relieved for all the spouses and families involved. But that's all it was to start: imagination. After all, I was just as much a hostage to serving my patients as anyone else.

Of course, with the mindset that I had to endure all types of work conditions to serve my patients, I became burned out by the ongoing changes and demands of the workplace. I was losing sleep, short-tempered, and felt hopeless. I could exercise or meditate to destress momentarily, but the problem was not going away. I was miserable.

The thing about being an employee is that you are responsible for the outcome, but you have no control over the process. I could either let the toll keep mounting, or I could at least control my own small process.

So I woke up, left my job, and decided to go full steam ahead on bringing medicine back to the hands of physicians. That would mean giving physicians the ability to practice medicine as we know it should be practiced. I wanted to help doctors find private practices that were owned and run by doctors so they could practice alongside the same people responsible for managing the practice. Starting a practice isn't for everyone, but joining one can be.

I have had my share of setbacks, doubts, and tears. But as a doctor, we're built to overcome. In the same way we stay up late charting or mulling over a differential diagnosis so that we can serve our patients, my new challenges were mere obstacles on my path to improve the lives of my friends and colleagues.

In my mission, I have helped physicians change course from feeling so burned out that they were ready to leave medicine entirely to rediscovering the rewarding career that we have all chosen. Practices choose to work with me over the well-established recruiting entities because they know what I stand for and that I will connect them with like-minded physicians out there.

And so I write this to my fellow physicians to let you know: I'm part of a cavalry that is here to bring medicine back into our hands, where it belongs. In this journey, I have met countless dedicated and creative physicians who embrace change and uncertainty and are fighting the same battle. We are here, and we will make sweeping changes.

My story is your story. You can join the movement in any capacity, whether that is through influencing politics, joining a physician-owned practice, or educating people with casual conversation. But no matter your ability, know that I am one of many who has arrived to take back medicine. The cavalry is here.

Author: Dr. Lara Hochman

Lara Hochman, MD, is a family medicine physician and advocate for fellow physicians' well-being amid rising burnout and dissatisfaction. Her own experiences led her to discover the ways physicians lost autonomy and how to reclaim their focus on helping patients. Since then, she has founded Happy Day Health, a boutique physician matchmaking agency that matches doctors with well-run, physician-owned private practices where they can avoid burnout and enjoy practicing medicine again.

She currently lives in Austin, Texas with her husband, two kids, and two fur babies. Follow her on Instagram: @happydaymd.

CHAPTER 13

CONNECTING AND **COLLABORATING** TO CREATE CHANGE

I was terminated. In the middle of a busy clinic day, with a full patient panel, I was called into the administrator's office and let go. I was no longer an employed physician in the group I'd been a part of, helped grow, and had an extensive loyal patient following for sixteen years.

I opened my now ex-employer's office door to my personal belongings haphazardly collected in a box at my feet. Shocked and tearful, I walked back to my work area and collected the remainder of my things, under my ex-employer's watchful eye. My charts were unfinished. My patients were left waiting. Without being given a chance to explain, say goodbye or communicate with anyone, my ex-employer escorted me out of the building. I felt awful, unsettled, and demoralized.

Thinking back, I now realize this experience was the catalyst that launched my transformational journey into entrepreneurship. That day, I took back control of my own life. For years, I had followed the path of least resistance, making my decisions within the formalized framework one follows to become a physician. Opportunities were presented, and I chose and moved forward, never really stopping to think about what it was I really wanted, or how I really wanted to spend my time and live my life.

Fast forward several months. I'd joined a new small private practice, and many of my patients had found and followed me. Each time I walked into a room and saw a familiar face, my heart swelled and filled with joy, a gift given.

Promised a certain salary, benefits, and partnership/ownership potential, I put my all into the business. I grew my patient panel. I allowed my schedule to be flexible, rounding and filling in as needed. I created social media platforms for the practice on Facebook, Instagram, and Google. I redid the outdated website—twice. I learned about search engine optimization and marketing and wrote all of the website, blogs, and social media posts. I came in early, stayed late, worked through lunch, and took on multiple administrative roles, consistently acting as an "owner." If a problem presented itself, I stepped up and fixed it.

Despite my efforts, my return on investment never materialized. I was asked to do more without any change in compensation. Finally, I thought, *What am I doing? Why am I spending all of my time promoting someone else's business?*

So I pivoted my efforts. I faced my fears, put myself out there, created my own website/blog, and set to work growing my own social media platforms. My twitter handle @PedsMamaDoc became my brand. My son helped create the logo. Just like that, I'd created a business brand platform on which to share my voice.

Connecting with other like-minded physicians through social media increased my innate passion and drive to support and lift up others. I was nicknamed a "shameless sharer" for tagging others on posts, articles, and any information relevant to physicians, medicine, and patient care. I consistently spread any information I truly believed in, working to educate, inspire, and support other physicians. Albeit unknowingly at first, I was finding my voice.

One afternoon I received a text from Dr. Marion Mass that read, "Do you have a minute to chat?"

"Sure," I replied. Forty-five minutes later I hung up the phone. I'd just spent my lunch hour talking with a fellow physician mom about our current fractured and broken healthcare system.

Connecting with Dr. Mass led me to learn about pharmacy benefit managers, group purchasing organizations, lobbying, and that the lack of transparency existing throughout our current healthcare system was purposefully created. I was now aware of existing legislation that allows nonphysicians to care for patients without completing the necessary education/training required to obtain a medical license. How, over the past two to three decades, third-party middlemen and government policies have inserted themselves into our sacred house, disrupting the patient-physician relationship and impeding access and the ability to actually receive care.

My interest piqued, I embraced my growing need to create change. I became an activated physician.

In September 2019, I wrote "To Extinguish Burnout, Bring Back Physician Autonomy." Accepted and published by KevinMD, it was shared over 8,000 times, republished in medical groups and journals, and even cited on Reddit.

I realized then that my voice matters. My words resonated with thousands of other physicians. I could spark conversation and discussion, ignite and further fan the flames toward much needed change. My article going viral gave me the courage to continue writing, to keep speaking up and putting myself out there.

I have since written articles for multiple platforms, built an extensive social media following, and created a blog with over 6,000 followers. Connecting with like-minded physicians advocating for change has led to speaking opportunities at conferences and on podcasts and to collaborating with Free2Care, Physicians Working Together, HPEC, SoMeDocs, AMWA's Gender Equity Task Force, MN Mental Health Advocates, TakeEMBack/TakeMedicineBack, and more. Most recently, I was interviewed on a local news station, filmed an episode as a guest pediatrician on *Kid Talk with Banana Girl* for *THE BIG EPIC SHOW* YouTube channel, and learned my work will be published in a soon-to-be released book, *Prevention of Burnout in Medicine: Multimedia Primer and Lifebook* by Dr. Brown Cares, LLC.

By believing in myself and saying yes to opportunities, I've found and grown my voice, my confidence, my platform, and my desire to reach other physicians. I recognize I can impact lives and create needed change. I've realized I am not alone, isolated in a silo with my beliefs. I now understand the importance of speaking up and the difference I can make in this world by doing so. I see potential and possibility for change everywhere. Through connection and collaboration, I've grown and nurtured a vast network of empowered change makers. I've found my people. I've embraced knowing that my network is my net worth, and it's just the beginning of what's yet to come.

Believe in possibility. Believe in yourself, your worth, your value, and your expertise. I challenge each and every one of you to activate—*find*, *own*, and *use your voice*.

Author: Dr. Christina Dewey, FAAP

Founder and CEO of PedsMamaDoc, LLC, Dr. Christina Dewey is a board-certified pediatrician; a fierce advocate for physicians, patients, children, mental health, and vaccines; and a published author. She has spoken at the Free2Care Conference and The Maternal Mental Health Summit, appeared as a guest on *Kid Talk with Banana Girl* on *THE BIG EPIC SHOW*, and was named a 2021 Top Doctor in *Minnesota Monthly* magazine. Dr. Dewey is also active in multiple grassroots physician advocacy groups and shares her insights, views, and ideas on her blog *PedsMamaDoc.com*.

She lives in Minneapolis, Minnesota with her husband, son, daughter, and two rescue dogs. Follow Dr. Dewey on Twitter: @PedsMamaDoc.

CHAPTER 14

THE THING TO FEAR
IS **FEAR**

I can still remember that phone call from my dad. His exact words were, "Your mother is no more." There was silence and disbelief, and then I hung up the phone. My mother had fallen suddenly about three days prior and was rushed to the hospital. She was in a coma and had brain swelling due to bleeding from a ruptured cerebral blood vessel. She was transferred to a specialist hospital, and the doctors did all they could, but she did not make it out. She was forty-eight years old.

I grew up in a big family with very hard-working parents, and I learned from an early age that I had to work hard to succeed in life. Both parents were hardly ever around, and whenever they showed up, there were a lot of distractions and so many people to share the attention. When my mother passed, I did exactly what I knew how to do best: I worked hard through medical school and residency. I told myself things would slow down and I would finally get a break when I started seeing my own patients.

However, when I finally achieved my goal of becoming an attending pediatrician and seeing my own patients, I was at a loss. It was not quite what I expected.

There was no time to connect or teach the patients like I wanted to. There were so many restrictions and rules on how I should be taking care of patients. Through medical school and residency, I was given pathways to follow and get desired results, and although these pathways are great in the fast-paced industry of medicine, I lost myself and my creativity.

In medical school, I was told on several occasions about the number of doctors who would be sued in the first year out of residency. That put an extra level of fear in me. I thought as long as I practiced evidence-based medicine according to the designed guidelines, I was safe. The patients were safe, insurance companies satisfied, and the lawyers away. So I constantly made sure my notes were perfectly done, and I was doing everything to make sure the patients felt taken care of. This led to more time spent doing paperwork and practicing fear-based medicine.

As you can imagine, the practice of fear-based medicine was exhausting and led to my burnout. I was always tired and started having frequent headaches. I did not have the strength or time to be there for my daughters. I was following the same path as my mother, and I needed help.

Not sure exactly what my options were, I searched online and started listening to podcasts about doctors who were branching out of medicine. As I searched, I entered into another cycle of overwhelm. There was a plethora of information, and everyone else seemed to be ten steps ahead. I bought more courses than I had the time to complete and attended so many free webinars that I was burned out.

Finally, I came across *The EntreMD Podcast*, which provided me with information and options I didn't realize I had. I was not aware of how much authority I had with my medical degree outside of the exam room. The podcast also helped me understand the power of taking small consistent action steps, so I stopped studying and started taking action.

However, this time the actions were not in the library or behind my computer—I needed to put myself out there. I tried on my own but made very little progress due to fear of failure and what people would say. After a few months of starting and stopping, I joined the EntreMD Business School.

At EntreMD, I met a community of doctors on the same journey. I realized that we all have the same fears, and the only way to move past our fears is to take action.

With coaching and a community cheering each other, I committed to one blog post and one YouTube video a week. Next, I needed to put myself out there and tell people what I was doing. This was the hardest for me. I still am not comfortable enough listening to myself talk, let alone letting the world know.

It took a lot of courage, but I did it. I started with my family and then on different social media outlets. Is it perfect? No, nor where I want it to be, but I am helping somebody and adding value. I am now officially a blogger and YouTuber, empowering parents to create sustainable healthy habits for their families.

I am putting in my miles, and I am getting better with each action step.

As I challenge myself and put myself out there via YouTube videos and blog posts, my confidence has increased. Yes, I'm still afraid, but my focus has changed and the fear is no longer stopping me. It's no longer about what people think of me but what I can do to serve and add value to someone else. I have shifted my focus from myself to impact, and my reason for doing it is now bigger. So I consistently show up—doing it afraid.

This confidence has translated to other areas of my life and how I show up. As I write this chapter, I am at the end of my contract at the practice where I work. I have the option to stay, but I have to move on because it has become uncomfortable staying in my comfort zone. I have negotiated a new contract so I can work part time on a comfortable income while positioning myself as an expert doing what I love and spending more time with my daughters. I have registered my business, Generational Wellbeing, and am working on creating online courses and coaching for parents.

A year ago, I would have stayed exactly where I was doing the same thing because I was comfortable, but not anymore. I now realize true success is on the other side of fear.

Author: Dr. Lum Frundi

Dr. Lum Frundi is a board-certified pediatrician and the founder of Generational Wellbeing, an online wellness service where she helps busy mothers create sustainable healthy habits so that they can change the narrative from disease to wellness. She has an active YouTube channel called *Generational Wellbeing* and has interviewed some amazing physicians on Instagram.

Dr. Frundi lives in Powder Springs, Georgia with her husband and two kids. Follow her on Instagram: @drlummd.

CHAPTER 15

FROM EXPERT TO
NOVICE AGAIN

Crimson blood spurts from the center of the ulcer. There is a palpable tension in the room, but I remain calm—I am an expert gastroenterologist. I inject epinephrine, and the white blanche feels familiar. I place the shiny metal clip across the vessel, hear it click, and the bleeding stops. Success!

This calm does not extend to all aspects of my life. The next day, I must call the CEO of a beauty company to collaborate on my business, and my heart is racing. I am a puddle. The introvert in me is terrified of conversation, and I do not want to embarrass myself. This is not about life or death, but fear creeps in because I am not an expert, and my ego is protecting me from harm.

I am creating an app to help women of color more easily find makeup. My entrepreneurial journey was born out of a desire to have autonomy, foster creativity, and follow a calling to help people feel seen in an industry that has ignored them. But I was paralyzed by fear and reluctant to start this journey because I did not know what I was doing and had no connections. I was a "nobody" in the beauty industry.

Then I thought to myself, *If a teenager on Instagram can become a billionaire in the cosmetics industry, why can't a bright, self-motivated, resourceful physician like me make it?* So I created a plan to make myself an expert and give myself the confidence I needed to start my business. I also had to train my ego to be vulnerable enough to learn the countless things I did not know.

I started with something doctors are good at: research. Once you have an idea, you need to investigate whether it is original, whether other companies have succeeded in this space, and who your competitors are. You also need to learn about your industry and the needs of your ideal customer. I read about the history of diversity in the beauty industry, makeup formulation, and the basics of building an app. I downloaded many apps, and I bought mountains of makeup to evaluate the products and go through the customer experience. I am drowning in makeup. But that is how I immersed myself in my craft.

I then focused on the journey of my ideal customer. I read their articles and joined online groups for women of color in order to understand their pain points. I talked to friends and acquaintances and asked questions on social media. Through these stories, I was able to feel the sting of sadness, anger, and embarrassment that my customers felt when they went to the store and were informed by the salesperson that there were no products available to purchase for their skin tone. Nothing. Just told to go home.

I gathered a lot of information, like you do in the first two years of med school. Now I needed real-life experience; I needed to network. I built a community on Instagram by creating a page focused on beauty for women of color. Soon, beauty brands and influencers were also interacting with my posts. My most exciting moment was when Miss Universe Australia reposted my Instagram post about how empowering it was to see her breaking the barriers of what beauty looks like. Through these interactions, I was no longer on the outside looking in!

To network further, I reached out to people who had common goals. I would recommend starting with smaller brands that share your mission. If you can genuinely promote a brand's product before reaching out, you are doing them a favor and they may be more likely to respond.

I have met some amazing people this way. One of my favorite encounters was with Aishetu Dozie, the founder of Bossy Cosmetics. I was inspired by her and the mission of her company and had promoted her products on my page. She gave me fantastic advice about entrepreneurship and offered to support me in whatever capacity she could. Imagine my surprise when I was listening to Guy Raz's podcast, *How I Built This*, months later and she was one of the guests. This is the podcast whose very first interview was with Spanx founder, Sara Blakely. I was even more surprised when I was perusing the list of "Oprah's Favorite Things" and saw Bossy Cosmetics' lipsticks as one of those items! I went from knowing no one in the industry to knowing this amazing rock star of a woman!

There is no better way to learn from experts than to hear their experiences. In addition to directly contacting them, I followed inspiring entrepreneurs on social media and read books and listened to podcasts where they documented their journeys. We always see the finished product, but we don't see the years of rejection, self-doubt, and hard work that it took the founder of a company to get there. It is helpful to hear how successful people stumbled into their businesses, took their first steps, and overcame adversity. As an additional step, formal business coaching has allowed me to get advice directly from experts and surround myself with a community of people who are pushing each other to succeed.

The entrepreneurial journey is hard when you feel like a "nobody," especially when you are used to being the calm, collected expert in the room. But you are not a "nobody." You have all the tools you need to become an expert, and even if you make a mistake, you have the breathing room to say, "No one will die…except maybe my ego."

Remember, if you made it through medical school and residency, you can do hard things. You can be vulnerable in a space where you do not have expertise, and you can be a successful entrepreneur.

Author: Dr. Priya Roy

Dr. Priya Roy is a board-certified gastroenterologist, a member of the ACG Women in GI Committee, and current vice-chair of internal medicine at a hospital. She is also the founder of EmpowerHue, a company that helps women of color more easily find makeup and skincare products. This business stemmed from her interests in medicine, science, beauty, and the desire to help people feel validated.

Dr. Roy resides in Columbus, Ohio with her husband and two children. You can find her on Instagram: @huesparkle.

CHAPTER 16

WHY NOT!
BECOMING WHO
YOU ARE

" It is with saddened hearts that we announce the passing of Dr. Z." Kind words and a description of his job duties were listed, followed by words that instantly made me want to vomit: "Dr. S will be the replacement until the position can be fulfilled." Dr. Z's contributions and the details of his career were diluted to several sentences, quickly followed by what amounted to a job posting.

I could not proceed as usual anymore. I'd blown past the anecdotes of my colleagues' divorce filings and the missed milestones of their children, and handled the letdown of metrics never to be met as if I had immunity. Reading the summation of Dr. Z's contributions watered down, I faced my own mortality as a *status quo physician.*

I had hit the wall that many others in medicine had seen for themselves—some things are just not worth it. I had been driving down a tunneled pathway that led to living with less intention and more burnout. I was betraying myself and could no longer compromise. I decided to make a change. I decided that I would just say no and set limits to things that detracted from my value.

I had allowed myself to become overleveraged at work, but changing my mindset changed everything. I prioritized my own terms and placed emphasis on rebalancing my goals. I started clarifying my time at work. I set limits on going into overdrive. I worked with the staff to balance out the scheduling of patients. I formed guidelines for patient management and visit expectations. I embraced telemedicine and bolstered these types of visits in my practice. My patients even began to report higher satisfaction scores and felt that they had better access to care.

These changes were my first successes. I had felt bound to schedules, patient satisfaction surveys, compensation models, and practice structures not in my control. Unlocking myself from those algorithms gave me the freedom to think about pursuits that added value to my life.

With a now restructured work environment, I sought out communities and held conversations with colleagues who appeared to be prioritizing their well-being. I learned how they began to make transitions that provided satisfaction. The journey has been profound. I found that all you have to do is dare to ask "Why not?" and then take the first step to prioritize yourself.

In medicine, prioritizing yourself seems counterintuitive. Altruism is taught from day one of medical school. Looking inward is sold as being less ambitious, smart, talented, or lazy. But it is not.

The essence of being a physician is commitment and consistency, and these qualities are hallmarks to success and achievement in both business and life. Surveying top business professionals and colleagues whom I admired, I found that they were both passionate and consistent. I realized, as a well-trained physician, I can achieve any goal I set.

Now that my perspective was rebalancing, I began to focus more on action. Shifting toward action, I accepted that life is rarely all or nothing. Life is dynamic. I learned how to stay fluid. I began to research and ask questions of various physician entrepreneurs. If something really piqued my interest, then I reached out via social media or email.

To my surprise, my colleagues were more than happy to help. My terror at stepping out of my comfort zone quickly subsided as I relearned a fundamental part of training: asking questions and gathering information. I also re-embraced that art of learning. I began to attend conferences and webinars that focused on a variety of topics that I found important and interesting.

As I drilled down on keeping myself whole, I reimagined the concept of productivity. I figured out what the important things were in my life and then built around that. I felt emboldened to prioritize hobbies, family, and time to hear my own thoughts.

In branching out, I also accepted that I would screw up some steps along the way. I extrapolated the wins from failure and rebounded. *Modify* and *pivot* became resounding lessons as I learned and adapted. I kept reminding myself that as a physician, I am trained to "figure it out" and generate solutions. I began to think as an entrepreneur. I believed in myself.

Shifting felt scary and anxiety-provoking, but complacency felt worse, so I pressed forward and refused to be stagnant. I've learned that our brains are triggered to calculate loss, making it easier to imagine what we stand to lose instead of what we stand to gain. Armed with this knowledge, I set in my mind the notion that plenty of fortuitous opportunities are available along my path. Anytime I became skittish, I would imagine my hindsight being 20/20 of all the things I could have said yes to: the seat at the table, more family time, turning a hobby into a business. I kept the courage to reach up on the shelf and take down what was best for me. I allowed myself to thrive.

I fueled my momentum with lots of grace. I gave myself the benefit of the doubt. I extended it to everyone and everything else— the wrong food in the takeout order or late patients—so why not for myself? And in moments of fear, I channeled gratitude and abundance.

The spirit of gratitude helped eliminate self-doubt. I see change as an opportunity. Whenever fear creeps in, I recall all the hard things accomplished. I remember that my training makes me adaptable and artful. I remember that I am both consistent and persistent.

I am grateful and content having left behind my fears and doubts. I have tasted wholeness and well-being. Both are quite fulfilling.

Author: Dr. Tia M. Guster

Dr. Tia Guster is a board-certified OB/GYN currently serving as the department head at Piedmont Newnan Hospital. She received her bachelor's degree and residency completion from Emory University and completed her medical degree from the University of North Carolina School of Medicine at Chapel Hill.

Dr. Guster is a proponent of Women's Health advocacy. She loves teaching and serves as a clinical preceptor. Outside the hospital, she enjoys running and creating a positive and affirming environment.

CHAPTER 17

CALLED AND "UNQUALIFIED"

As I watched a group of doctors in long white coats walk past me and registered nurses in their white scrubs fixated on their computers on wheels, I was dreaming. In my second year of residency, I was dreaming of what life could look like if I had control.

Control meant impacting people in the unique way that only I could. Only one and a half years into training, I had already witnessed doctors' lack of control. You go through this intense training and rack up six figures of debt, just to live out someone else's dream.

The salary was great, but it was not enough for me. I wanted to live out my own dream. I wanted to become more than a doctor, and I knew to do that, I could not contain myself within the walls of a clinic or hospital forever.

I didn't know where to start, so I went to Google. I found Jim Rohn, and I read the single most powerful quote that I have ever heard: "Work harder on yourself than you do on your job." From that quote, I learned to develop habits, such as creating dedicated time for prayer and exercise, weekly goal setting, and journaling. By serving myself first, I gained a strong desire to serve my patients even more.

I started to make short videos on Instagram on mindset and exercise. My first video took about three hours, and I must have done about twenty takes! I called myself Dr. J because I sort of felt like a rebel and did not want to give my residency program a bad rap.

When I got accepted into a sports medicine fellowship, I felt pressured and scared because in only one year I would become an attending. I was scared of becoming *just* a doctor. Other times, I thought maybe I was just a doctor after all, but the thought of not utilizing *all* of me to serve people in that unique way only I could scared me even more.

Midway into fellowship, I made a goal for the first quarter of the year. My goal for each month of the first quarter was to reach out to one doctor who was authentically impacting their people and monetizing it in the process. The first doctor I spoke to was Dr. E.

She asked me, "Well, what makes you unique?" Huh? I did not know what made me unique. I knew I loved fitness and hated the constant pill prescription associated with chronic disease, so I thought, *Well, maybe I could help prevent that with exercise and lifestyle changes.*

Next, I reached out to Dr. Z, who advised me to get a business coach, preferably a doctor. I had never heard of the term "business coach" before. She gave me some referrals, one being Dr. Una.

Then I spoke to Dr. R, who also advised me to get a business coach. *Okay, God! I hear you! I need a business coach.* But a business coach sounded like a lot of money, and I was merely a fellow.

At the end of the first quarter, I received an email about the Leverage & Growth Summit, a virtual conference for physician entrepreneurs. I thought I could certainly find a physician business coach there. My introductory post on their Facebook group went something like this: "Hi, I am Dr. J. I'm so happy to be here. I'm looking for a physician business coach!"

Almost instantly, I got comments stating that I should reach out to Dr. Una. That name sounded familiar. I kept scrolling down the Facebook group to read the rest of the introductions, and I stopped at this beautiful Black woman with the most infectious smile. I stopped scrolling and stared at her. It was as if she was telling me, "Hello, I am the person who is going to help you step into all that God has created you for." Long story short, I closed my eyes and hit submit to enroll in the EntreMD Business School.

So who am I now? I am an official YouTuber. I release weekly content on mindset and exercise. In order to stay ahead, I batch my videos to ensure that I have a new video being released every single week. I have a virtual assistant who helps with my social media content on Instagram, but prior to that, I was overwhelmed from doing it all. Now my rule of thumb is, if I hate it, I delegate it!

I have developed the habit of asking. I used to feel unworthy of asking to speak on other people's platforms because I was still in training. I also did not think I was an eloquent speaker because I said "um" a lot. Learning to ask has landed me guest spots on over fifteen podcasts and has created more exposure for my business. Now I see every speaking opportunity as a chance to also work on my "ums" as I lead with the power thought, "I own my ums!"

The story of Gideon from the Bible has helped me embrace my value as well as my identity as a rising entrepreneur. God assigned Gideon to lead the Israelite army in a battle against the more formidable Midianite army. However, Gideon was the youngest in his family and part of the weakest tribe. He questioned his ability multiple times. Despite these feelings, Gideon led anyway, and he was able to win so great a victory that the Israelites had peace for forty years!

I felt like entrepreneurship was a calling, but like Gideon, I felt unqualified because I was still a trainee. I have since learned that God does not call the qualified; he qualifies the called. I am called to do this work. There are people who need me, so even though I have limiting beliefs, I do the work anyway. I have since learned that I was already qualified. I just had to step into it.

Author: Dr. Janeeka Benoit

Dr. Janeeka Benoit, better known as Dr. J, is a board-certified internal medicine and sports medicine physician. She is a locum physician, which allows her the flexibility to travel and create her life around her work. She started her business, MedFitDO, shortly after graduating from fellowship, serving as a health and fitness coach to help busy professional women become the architect of their lives through mental fitness. Dr. J is also the host of the *Reinventing Fitness* podcast.

Dr. J lives in Nashville, Tennessee but proudly reps Brooklyn, New York any day. You can find her on Instagram: @medfitdo.

CHAPTER 18

CREATIVE **LICENSE**

Dare to Dream Differently

My medical assistant knocked lightly on my half-open office door, the signal that my patient was ready for me in the exam room.

"Okay, thanks," I said, smiling up from my computer. But inside, I had a sense of dread. I had noticed it more and more lately. I loved my patients, so why did I dread that knock on the door?

I went in to see the patient, spoke to and examined her, and determined that she had a gallbladder problem. I delivered my well-rehearsed speech about gallbladder disease and cholecystectomy and signed her up for surgery.

There was something about it all that was wearing on me: the scripted conversations with patients, listening to their complaints through a lens of pattern recognition, and sorting them into neat categories. *(Does he have a hernia, or a strained muscle? Does she have symptomatic cholelithiasis, or an ulcer?)* My patients were so much more than their surgical diagnoses; they were multifaceted individuals. Often, their biggest problems were not even their surgical ones.

At the same time, my role as their doctor seemed to have been stripped of its human component. All too often, I felt like a cog in the medical wheel, there to provide the standard of care and document it, with time for nothing more. Even writing patient notes had been largely reduced to clicking checkboxes.

I should mention at this point that I have always been a creative person. As a girl, I loved making art and writing short stories. In high school and college, however, I gradually came to believe that being a physician was the ultimate career, never mind whether it completely aligned with my strengths. If I *could* make it as a doctor, I *should*.

And so, I did. I put my head down and graduated from college with excellent grades while playing varsity soccer. I was accepted to medical school and joined the military to fund my training while serving my country. I completed residency and fellowship. I became board certified. I taught residents and students. I took care of the sickest of the sick in a Level I Trauma and Burn Center. Fulfillment seemed to be always just around the corner. *If I wasn't happy now, there must be something wrong with me.*

I would later realize that years of prioritizing my medical training over my creative gifts had led me to this place of unfulfillment. With no outlet, my creative energy had begun to eat away at me.

The other factor weighing on me was much more concrete. At the start of my training, I had no one to care for but myself. Now

I was a single mother of three young children. I realized that my work *had to* energize me, because otherwise I would have nothing left for my kids, who were my first priority.

Even though I sensed the need for change, I didn't truly consider stepping away from clinical medicine until I hit a crisis point.

When I neared completion of my military obligation, I began my search for my first civilian position. I made a list of potential practices, completed a few phone interviews, and interviewed in person at my top choice. I was invited back for a second interview, which seemed to go well.

I was in my office when I got the call. I was not being offered the job. I went from feeling numb to confused to hurt. *Had I made that bad of an impression on the second visit?*

After nursing my pride, I went back to the job search drawing board, adding more potential practices to my list. Until it hit me. I didn't actually *want* to do this.

For so long, I hadn't bothered to ask myself what I really wanted. Somehow, the closed door on what I thought was my best job opportunity put everything in perspective. I had options. I could choose to spend my days doing something that energized me.

At first, I researched popular nonclinical jobs for physicians, but few had much appeal. So I took another approach—I allowed myself to dream. *What type of work excites me? What fills my cup rather than empties it?* I reflected on how, ever since I was young, I thrived on creating. Whether it was a scrapbook page, a painting, or a story, I loved taking a project from idea to reality, using my hands and brain in concert.

During my training, I had walked through several difficult life events, including the loss of my mother. I was reminded through these trials that the messages I focused on had a great impact on the outcomes in my life. I began a practice of hand lettering, writing out the messages I wanted to focus on and placing them where I would see them. Both the process of lettering and the visual reminders I created helped to set the soundtracks for my life. Now I began to dream of sharing this power with others.

In early 2021, I founded Words of Hope Designs LLC. Its mission is to spread hope through hand-lettered art. Like most physicians, I had little business knowledge when I started. But I took baby steps, using the free training the Small Business Administration offered and watching online tutorials. I joined the EntreMD Business School and gained a tribe of other physician entrepreneurs to learn and grow with.

In about six months, my business has gone from concept to reality. I sell my artwork in a local storefront, on Etsy, and from my website. I have sold over 120 art prints, completed ten commissions, and been featured on three podcasts and two blogs. I earned a spot in the Emerging Makers tent at one of the largest craft fairs in my state. I am leading a creativity workshop at an upcoming conference for female physicians and preparing to launch my YouTube channel. Perhaps most importantly, I am doing work that is meaningful, fulfilling, and energizing and that also allows me to walk my kids to and from school each day.

Imagine looking at the things you dread about your current job through a lens of curiosity, asking "What if?" rather than believing you need to squeeze yourself into a broken mold. Imagine feeding your dreams instead of keeping them pushed down inside of you. Imagine finding a tribe to support you.

I'm here to tell you it's possible. It's out there. It's yours for the taking.

Author: Dr. Joanna Cranston

Dr. Joanna Cranston is a general surgeon by training and a US Army veteran. She left clinical medicine in 2021 to pursue her dream of spreading hope through words and art. As the founder and CEO of Words of Hope Designs, she creates hand-lettered art, speaks about the transformative power of our thoughts, and teaches hand lettering. She was also a featured speaker at the Authenticity, Courage, and Empowerment (ACE) Conference for Women Physicians in 2022.

Dr. Cranston lives in Clarksville, Tennessee with her three children, who inspire her to embrace creative thinking. You can follow her on Instagram: @wordsofhopedesigns.

CHAPTER 19

DESPITE ALL **ODDS**

F ear of failure and self-doubt almost changed the trajectory of
my life more than once.

My dream to become a physician seemed impossible as a
first-generation teenage immigrant who did not speak English
when I came to the United States. The journey was long and hard,
but despite all odds, I became the first person in my family to
graduate from high school and the first physician.

It has been my goal to make a difference in the lives of patients
and their families. But although I have enjoyed working with my
colleagues and caring for patients over the years, missing out on
family and kids' activities was difficult. With an increasing work-
load, emails, messages, and late-night charts, it seemed as though
I could not keep up.

I found myself frequently tearing up on my drive to work after
leaving my crying baby at day care. My kids were the last ones to
be picked up since I was usually running behind in the clinic. I am
thankful for my husband, who was working hard and tried to help,
but there were times we could not pick our children up when the

day care called saying our kids were sick or hurt. It was a struggle finding childcare during the holidays. I sometimes dreaded going on vacation or long weekend trips because I would be very busy before and after.

Deep down, I wished to have more time with my family and to create a legacy. As physicians, we neglect our health and relationships to help others, and I was constantly tired, stressed out, and exhausted.

I remember the first time someone suggested real estate investing several years ago—I quickly rejected the notion. I was too busy with work and kids. It felt too risky, and I had heard horror stories about real estate investing. Besides, I did not have the money due to medical school debt, and I did not come from a wealthy family. Having worked at low-wage jobs and being a first-generation immigrant from a third world country, I worked hard to save. I knew nothing about finances or investing and taking risks.

However, there is usually an opportunity cost for not taking some risks. "I wish mommy could be here today on my birthday," I heard my son say as he reenacted how my younger daughter had said these words while she waited for me to come home from work on her special day. I felt a pang of guilt while gently kissing her on the living room couch that night. I knew I needed to create a work-life balance so that I did not miss out on being with my kids while they were little.

The COVID-19 pandemic exacerbated tight schedules and childcare challenges, but it was the wake-up call I needed to understand how short and unpredictable life can be. I did not want my little one going to day care before being vaccinated against COVID-19, so I decided to resign from my senior physician position and changed to per diem so that I could have more flexibility and spend time with my kids.

I first saw what was possible when I witnessed several physicians starting businesses and investing to take back their autonomy and create the life they wanted. At this point, I still felt overwhelmed with analysis paralysis. However, instead of feeling behind and discouraged, I decided to focus on learning and finding every opportunity I could to continue working toward my goals. I signed up for several courses, coaching programs, and connected with like-minded people. Having a strong why and mindset shift was essential in making the progress. It helped me persevere, especially when I faced struggles and challenges in my real estate investing and entrepreneurial journey.

Focusing on the next essential step propelled me onward when I felt overwhelmed having to juggle so many responsibilities. Now remote real estate investing and managing have helped me become more resourceful. For instance, I have learned to leverage teams, technology, and systems to automate processes to work toward time freedom.

I enjoy seeing my personal transformation and creating vacation getaways for families so that they can create memories. My vision is to create large wellness and retreat centers for physicians, healthcare professionals, and nonprofits. It is my desire to advocate for physician wellness, help them live their best lives, and practice medicine the way they see fit.

I am thankful that my work now allows me to homeschool my younger daughter and pick up my son early from school. My kids enjoy surprise stops at different playgrounds and restaurants. I feel blessed to savor the little moments in life with them, like extra sleep, snuggles, and laughter.

"The sand is so soft and white!" I remember my kids yelling as they jumped up and down on the white powder sand at the private beach at our vacation home. It was a memorable trip I will not soon forget.

I want to continue to show my kids and others what is possible. I feel privileged to be able to help fellow physicians and friends learn real estate investing or business to help them achieve their goals. The reward of reaching for bigger goals is the growth journey and who you become in the process of tackling fears, doubts, struggles, and challenges.

I am proud to say my daughter did not have to wait for me to come home this year for her birthday. Our family had a wonderful getaway together and enjoyed beautiful nature while celebrating her special day.

If your entrepreneurial dream comes true, how would it impact you, your family, and your community? As physicians, we have done many hard things and overcome many challenges. Invest in yourself first and see how once-seemingly impossible goals can become possible. Together, we will create a greater ripple effect on each other and our community as we continue to grow and celebrate our best lives.

Author: Dr. Amy Hung

Dr. Amy Hung is a board-certified physician in family medicine and lifestyle medicine. She is the CEO and founder of Cherished Stays vacation home rentals, creating excellent stay experiences for guest families, friends, small masterminds, or retreat groups in beautiful places. She also helps physicians and those interested in real estate investing.

Dr. Hung has two young kids and enjoys traveling with family. You can join her private Facebook group: Invest To Impact MD.

SECTION I AUTHORS

Dr. Weili Gray

Dr. Nwando Anyaoku

Dr. Nerissa S. Bauer

Dr. Michele Johnson

Dr. Cheruba Prabakar

Dr. Recha Bergstrom

Dr. Amanda C. Adkins

Dr. Judit Andrea Staneata

Dr. Tamara Beckford

Dr. Lara Hochman

Dr. Kamilah M. Williams

Dr. Christina Dewey, FAAP

Dr. Lum Frundi

Dr. Janeeka Benoit

Dr. Priya Roy

Dr. Joanna Cranston

Dr. Tia M. Guster

Dr. Amy Hung

Dr. Jessica Daigle

STARTUPS

One of the biggest rewards of starting a business is the impact it has on the people it serves.

Think of the impact a primary care private practice can have—thousands and tens of thousands of patients who experience compassionate evidence-based care by an expert. Think about all the chronic illnesses that don't lead to long-term complications or the chronic illnesses that are avoided altogether because of education on lifestyle changes—all because one person said yes to launching the practice. The same applies if they are coaches, speakers, founders of nonprofit organizations, and so forth. The ripple effect of a successful business is profound.

The understanding of this fact makes the following statistic intolerable. A Harris Poll conducted in December 2020 revealed that 61 percent of Americans have an idea of starting a business, but the overwhelming majority of them (92 percent) never turn their idea into reality. *Ninety-two* percent.

This chapter is full of stories of doctors who are part of the 8 percent whose ideas are now reality! They will inspire you to own your ideas and follow the steps to start. The best part is that these businesses are having positive ripple effects in society already. See for yourself.

CHAPTER 20

AUTHENTICALLY ME

I can confidently share this now. I'm done with hiding who I am.

I was a talented and multi-passionate person, even before becoming a wife, doctor, and mother. (Many of us were—it's why we got into medical school.) Before I hit the age of ten, I had launched a newspaper from my fourth-grade classroom, coded websites, and even ran my parents' motel. I didn't have fears of success, failure, or judgment back then. I just had a spark mixed with grit and the desire to do and overcome. In early adulthood, I effortlessly organized communities, led nonprofit organizations, and fundraised. I did this work not because I had to check it off an action list, but because I loved it and gravitated toward making a mark on the world.

These skills and the unwavering belief that my calling was to be a physician landed me acceptance into medical school. I didn't realize it then, but how I spent my time before medical school broadly defined who I once was. Medical training and "adulting" usurped my existence to grow into who I needed to become.

You see, I needed all of my bandwidth to handle the transitions of young adulthood: to graduate medical school, become a mother of twins while in residency, and then an attending physician while navigating out of burnout. During those thirteen years, the entrepreneur in me had been hiding and begging to reenter the world. She would peek her head out every few months and nudge me to see if it was time to start a practice, but I silenced her desire because I wanted to survive. Eventually, I felt the burden of silencing my spirit.

I remember the start of 2020 being perfect. My daughters were five and proving to be awesome kids (phew, I hadn't yet ruined them!). My husband and I finally felt normal—we slept, socialized, and even went out into the world. I was settling into my second year at a fantastic practice with great colleagues and leadership. I also began participating in organized medicine and physician advocacy efforts. I felt healed from the massive burnout and heartache I had experienced at the start of my attending career. I was content and enjoying life. Picture perfect, yet it felt off.

I felt strange without a goal to reach or a deadline to overcome. I tried to channel my energy toward learning new hobbies—playing tennis, piano, gardening, and running. I did more "girls' night outs" and "trips." I was figuring out how to coast because I had arrived at the dream. But anytime my spirit wanted more, my brain just whispered, "It's too much effort; you'll be miserable," so I would bury the desires. But it hurt.

Then in March 2020, the COVID-19 pandemic started. I worked as a physician for a hotel and resort company in Orlando, Florida.

The world shut down, tourism plummeted, theme parks closed, and Orlando turned into a ghost town.

How would we transition to virtual care? How would we triage and treat COVID-19? I found myself on social media and connected with colleagues to find solutions. I joined the "virtual doctor's lounge," and my intrapreneurial skills kicked in. We jumped light-years ahead to take on the shutdown.

The practice figured out a new normal. The dust settled, and Florida's emergency orders were in effect, so I took obesity care online. While my patients were furloughed, they lost a grand total of 1,600 pounds. I effectively treated people from the comfort of their homes. This sparked a passion within—I wanted my own obesity medicine clinic. But how? While the world was still semi-shut down and my calendar wide open, the entrepreneur in me decided it was time to figure it out.

So I went back to my "virtual doctor's lounge" (i.e., social media groups) and connected with doctors to create the "side gig" of my dreams. Begrudgingly, I created my LLC and got my USPS mailbox —small wins. I spoke to EHR vendors and found a location.

I took these actions with lots of apprehension. I kept feeling as if every step needed to be precisely dosed. Naysaying ran through my mind. "The EHR vendors aren't going to want to deal with a small practice." "Banks will know I don't have experience." "Can I really be employed and also have a practice?" Every step of the way, I felt immense discomfort and felt alone. Then one day, I came across a post about *The EntreMD Podcast*. It was love at first listen.

I felt understood by Dr. Una. She boasted of a community of doctors like myself. I had felt broken before. Why did I want to do more when everything was perfect? Why couldn't I just be happy "being"? Didn't entrepreneurship mean sacrifices and being away from my family? I had just left that life. Why would I reenter? But Dr. Una told me I could practice medicine on my terms. She reminded me of my strengths. What if she was right?

I joined the EntreMD Business School. I learned a framework to accelerate my business on my terms. I became crystal clear on my vision and created the obesity medicine practice of my dreams. I learned to accept that discomfort and negative emotions are simply a part of growth. I now live in a world of doing, and the EntreMD community is a source of strength. The version of me I once knew before medicine lives again. I enjoy my employed position, have my "side gig" obesity medicine practice, and enjoy having freedom for my family. I now work for myself and show up where I want, from medical society meetings to PTA events. I accept positions on editorial boards. I even "openly" participate on social media. My bandwidth has been upgraded.

The woman I now am has drastically changed. I no longer feel broken. Instead, I see myself as I've always been—an entrepreneur who just happens to be a doctor. I'm authentically me.

Author: Dr. Nikita Bhakta Shah

Dr. Nikita Bhakta Shah is a board-certified family medicine and obesity medicine physician, as well as a certified life coach. She loves helping her patients lose weight, gain health, and transform into their best selves. As such, she founded Weight Sense Lake Nona, an obesity medicine practice in Orlando, Florida. One of her greatest achievements involves her work in modernizing Florida's obesity medicine rules to allow for weight care to be accessible via telehealth.

When she is not practicing medicine, Dr. Shah enjoys experiencing the magic of Orlando with her family. She can be found on Instagram: @nikitashahdo.

CHAPTER 21

OWN YOUR **DREAM**

Stepping Out Despite Uncertainty

H ere I was, a board-certified pediatric pulmonologist and sleep medicine physician in a prestigious academic institution. I was used to referring to myself by these titles, but I recently didn't feel as confident. Even though I knew I added value to my hospital, mentored trainees, led projects, published papers, and presented on national platforms, it didn't seem to be enough. The more I accomplished, the more I felt like I was living someone else's dream.

It was hard for people to understand this, and I felt some guilt at my sense of discontentment. It was hard to put words to my feelings. The best way I could describe this uneasiness is using the analogy of restless leg syndrome (RLS), a sleep-related disorder. RLS is an uncomfortable sensation in the lower extremities, occurs at bedtime, is aggravated by rest, and is relieved by movement. Classically, we ask patients to describe the discomfort in their own words. Like a patient with RLS, I was the only one in the position to articulate this discomfort, yet the words eluded me. I knew I needed to move and take action; otherwise, the restlessness would continue.

Once I identified these symptoms, it was time to pivot. I had a dream, and my current trajectory would not take me to my destination. I was being called to more and had no clue what "more" was, but I was bent on discovering it.

I would never have considered myself discontent or self-centered, but I realized I had to be both to live a life of impact. I was happily married and had two beautiful kids. I had seemingly achieved it all: I was the friend, colleague, doctor, teacher, advocate, healer, and mentor I had always dreamed I would be. However, the satisfaction I was hoping to achieve was just not there. I realized I had stopped having big dreams, that I had settled.

I had worked hard and achieved these goals but could not clarify what was next. I looked at my life in ten, twenty, and thirty years and couldn't imagine doing the same thing. So I decided to permit myself to dream again, to envision a life beyond where I was. I was scared, uncertain, and bombarded by feelings of self-doubt. Yet, I decided to trust my instincts, to listen to the discomfort and restlessness I experienced. I realized these were symptoms that I was being called to more.

Despite my dreams, the fears did not go away; in fact, they intensified. Where would I start? What was I trying to achieve? What would people say? How could I impact lives beyond the hospital setting? How would I continue to mentor trainees while helping busy professional moms thrive? What would the time commitment involve? At this point, I had two choices: to either let all the unknowns paralyze me to the end of inaction or to start taking action from where I was. I decided I would figure out the logistics as I went along.

As soon as I decided to pursue my dreams, I realized I needed a community. I needed restless people with big dreams like me. The world became small with the COVID-19 pandemic, and my community grew. I invested in books, courses, podcasts, and webinars. I joined several Facebook groups and communities of like-minded people, including the EntreMD Facebook group.

With the help of these communities and many introspections, I identified my values of significance, faith, community, impact, and encouragement. Although entrepreneurship was not one of my core values, I realized that entrepreneurship skills were critical to living out my purpose. This prompted me to join the EntreMD Business School (EBS), designed for physician entrepreneurs. I had no background knowledge of building a business, I knew this would be a steep learning curve, but I was excited to embark on this journey. I had a group of phenomenal EBS classmates who were now part of my tribe. Finally, I was owning my dream and equipping myself to accomplish it.

I am so glad I decided not to settle for just okay. I have experienced growth, mindset change, and success as an entrepreneur. In the EntreMD Business School, I have found a group of extraordinary physicians who have inspired and motivated me to get out of my comfort zone. I have articulated my dream better and generated well-defined goals.

I had a vision where busy professional women and their children prioritized sleep as a critical aspect of their health and wellness, enabling them to reach their fullest potential. My tool for achieving this goal was the knowledge and skills learned at EBS. My first step was to establish my physician brand as a sleep medicine expert. Unfortunately, no one knew about me or what I did, and few people understood how sleep deprivation affected their health and wellness—I needed to change that. I refused to be my world's best-kept secret, which meant putting myself out there.

From the moment I said yes, my growth has been exponential, and there have been so many milestones to celebrate on this journey. I founded Restful Sleep MD, using my expertise in course creation to launch my online sleep program, and have even been paid to create sleep courses for sizable online companies. I have taken advantage of social media and other networks to introduce myself to the world and create an awareness of sleep's impact on parents and their children. I have had the opportunity to speak on various platforms, including podcasts, YouTube channels, webinars, collaborations with other entrepreneurs on workshops, and other training sessions. I also recently contributed a sleep article featured in an online parenting magazine.

So much has happened, and I know this is just the beginning. My passion is emerging as a profitable business, but more importantly, I have had people reach out to me with testimonials of how much better they feel since being more intentional about their sleep. I am excited that I decided to own my dream and step out despite the uncertainty.

Author: Dr. Funke Afolabi-Brown

Dr. Funke Afolabi-Brown is a triple board-certified pediatric pulmonologist and sleep medicine physician. She is the founder of Restful Sleep MD, a company that helps busy professional women prioritize sleep to thrive and reach their fullest potential. She is a speaker, an educator, and a coach with an active YouTube channel called *Dr. Funke Brown*. Finally, Dr. Afolabi-Brown is on the medical advisory board for Baby Center, is a member of the American Academy of Sleep Medicine and the American Thoracic Society, and has presented on national and international platforms.

She lives in Maple Glen, Pennsylvania with her husband and two children. You can find her on Instagram: @restfulsleepmd.

CHAPTER 22

JUST **START**

H ave you ever felt like you needed to do more in life? I had
that feeling for quite some time, but I didn't know what it
meant. I had wanted to be a physician since I was a kid. Now I was
working in my chosen profession, changing lives. However, I felt
like it wasn't enough.

I was dissatisfied with my situation at the time. Initially, I
thought it was due to my job, so I changed employers. After a year, I
had the same feeling again. I realized it was not the job—it was me.
I realized that I needed to do more; I just didn't know what to do. I
started to do more volunteer work, but that didn't satisfy the feeling.

Around that time, I started to listen to podcasts. After binge
listening to podcasts like *The EntreMD Podcast* by Dr. Una and
Online Marketing Made Easy by Amy Porterfield, I realized that I
love my patients, but I could reach more people through a podcast.

So I started a podcast titled, *Back on Track: Overcoming Weight
Regain*. It was harder than I thought. You hear stories of how people
started their podcast in less than thirty days, but for me, it took
three months to actually release the first podcast episode. *Fear*

stopped me from starting: the fear of failure, the fear of no one listening, the fear of criticism, and the fear of being imperfect. I was supposed to release my podcast in May, but I pushed it back to June and then July.

This might have gone on forever if it wasn't for my accountability partner. She encouraged me to make a "save the date" post, and the next day I posted it at the EntreMD live event. Once I hit send, it was out in the world, and I knew I couldn't let people down. I worked tirelessly to record and put the first episode together. On July 1, 2021, I released my first episode.

There are three things that I have learned on this journey that helped me overcome the fear of starting: (1) believe, (2) take action, and (3) stop comparing myself.

1. Believe

I am not sure when I became so self-conscious and started second-guessing myself. Maybe it started as a child, a teenager, or even in medical school. When I look back at my life, there are times when I am impressed with the perseverance and resiliency that I showed to overcome challenges. However, when it came to starting my business and my podcast, that same attitude of overcoming challenges at all costs was not there.

It took me some time to get to a place where I believed that I could actually pull this off. I realized that if I could learn complex subjects like neurological pathways, I could learn to do a podcast. Once I started believing that this was possible, my attitude and demeanor changed, and I started to build momentum.

2. Take Action

Next, I started to take action. First, I started with research. I went online and joined three different podcast online courses, purchased a podcast journal, and listened to countless podcast episodes about building your podcast. I did so much research that I got stuck in research mode. I enjoyed learning what to do, but to actually do it was difficult for me. I found myself delaying my release date because I thought I still needed to do more research.

I was so blessed to have an accountability partner who helped me out. We met every week and talked about our progress, challenges, and goals for the next week. She helped me list out what I needed to do. By listing out the steps, it allowed my brain to step out there and take action. I was able to complete the weekly tasks and see progress in my podcast business.

3. Stop Comparing Myself

Although I was feeling good about taking action, I just couldn't stop comparing myself to what other people were doing, even though they had been doing this for many years at that point. When I looked at what they had accomplished, I would get discouraged.

Eventually, I realized that comparing myself with someone else is a waste of time and energy. When I stopped comparing myself, I felt so much better. I was able to overcome my perfectionist ways and I realized that it is not going to be "perfect," but it will be good enough.

Russell Branson (Co-founder of Click Funnels) said, "If I hadn't done the first forty-five episodes, I never would have gotten to episode forty-six, where I hit my stride. That's why it's so essential to start publishing your show now, even when you're not good at it. In the process of doing your show, you will find your voice." Once I realized this, I was able to see my podcast business as a journey and realize that with every episode I am learning what works, tweaking my business, and growing.

Since I released my podcast, my life has changed. I have had over 1,000 downloads in the first six months. I have been invited to speak on different podcasts. I even spoke at the Georgia American Society for Metabolic and Bariatric Surgeons. I was honored as being *Atlanta Business Chronicle's* "40 under 40." All of these accomplishments wouldn't have happened if I didn't start.

You may be thinking to yourself, she must be an anomaly; I can never do what she did. Well, you are wrong. You can do it, and you will do more! You just need to put fear behind you and start. Know that you have got this and that the world needs to hear what you have to say!

Author: Dr. Alicia Shelly

Dr. Alicia Shelly is a board-certified internal medicine/obesity medicine physician and the lead physician for Wellstar Douglasville Medical Center. She started a weekly podcast and YouTube channel titled *Back on Track: Overcoming Weight Regain*, as well as earned features on Shape.com, *Upscale* magazine, and many different podcasts. Finally, she is the medical director for Hope Missions 360, which delivers medical care to the underserved in the United States and Caribbean.

Dr. Shelly is also a fitness enthusiast who has completed six marathons and is training for her first IRONMAN in fall of 2022. She lives in Atlanta, Georgia and can be found on Instagram: @drshellymd.

CHAPTER 23

CREATING THE MINDSET OF A **SUCCESSFUL** PHYSICIAN ENTREPRENEUR

G rowing up, I was influenced by my parents, who were serial entrepreneurs. I remember the first business they had, which they named after me: DD Stores. It was a retail store that also served as a social lounge. I helped with daily business tasks, such as restocking shelves, bookkeeping, and making sure our clients had great customer service. I developed a passion for business and started to learn lessons around the ups and downs of entrepreneurship.

Years later, I became a typical busy medical student, working hard and studying around the clock to achieve my degree. My life was full of exciting opportunities to learn science, but being naturally curious, I soon realized that I needed to have other life experiences and interests to explore other parts of my brain. So I created my first business in transportation, which became my escape from the monotony of studying. I was excited and thrilled about the challenges of each day: managing my staff, dealing with customers, troubleshooting systems. In addition, I developed a fashion business dealing in bespoke couture for discerning clientele.

I believe that combining business and study in this way made me a more complete individual. My happiest times were spent engaging with business vendors, colleagues, or clients; hashing out a sale; or completing a business deal. However, as my medical training intensified, I had to concentrate on it alone so I could graduate with excellent grades. My businesses were put on hold.

After more than twenty-five years of training to become an internist, nephrologist, hypertension specialist, and developing multiple titles such as a researcher, assistant professor, wife, and mother of multiple children, I appeared to be successful to the outside world, but a big part of me was lost. Slowly, other forces at play began to creep up: the responsibilities of maturity and the lure and comfort of a predictable paycheck every two weeks. I settled for a "robotic" lifestyle of shuttling between work and then home and then work again.

Over time, boredom set in as I was forced to live this toxic robotic lifestyle. This was particularly challenging as an immigrant in a foreign country, far away from my support system and having to move across multiple states in pursuit of higher learning opportunities. During these transitions, I came across mentors and allies, but there were also many foes and haters along the way who made it their primary mission to destroy themselves as well as all in their path. At some point, I decided it was time to make drastic changes.

Out of the ashes, the phoenix arose. I started a period of self-development, self-improvement, and took several leadership courses. I learned how to identify those who were in alignment with my values and made tough decisions to leave toxic work environments, friendships, and even relocate once again. I read several books and learned new habits to reinforce forgotten old ideas. I made the decision to become a serial entrepreneur and gain financial freedom without sacrificing my family or compromising my values.

What does this mean? This means to become present and aware of the choices that you have as a physician and decide to become an entrepreneur. Physicians typically have more choices to earn and live a fulfilled life but for a variety of reasons—including fear of the unknown, feelings of inadequacy, and procrastination—choose to limit themselves. I have come to understand that fear is universal because all highly successful individuals must work through their fears by taking action.

First, I eliminated limiting beliefs that physicians cannot own successful businesses, that physicians do not have the skillset to run a business, or that they should not make money in a business. I realized that many of the skills required for business—including great communication and listening—are equally crucial for physicians to maintain excellent physician-patient relationships.

I also realized that physicians need to let go of the idea that more training is required and recognize that the desire to obtain yet another certificate or degree may be a form of procrastination. Often, physicians, who already have, on average, more than ten extra years of education than the average person of similar age, feel the need to get more training to excel at whatever venture they decide to pursue.

Next, I set up clear goals with the end in mind: What do I want to create? What is the end product going to be, or what do I want to achieve? Who can help me achieve these goals? Examples of tools to set up clear goals include writing in a journal daily and creating voice notes. Or breaking big goals into smaller tasks and asking for help when you have tasks that require different skills than you possess. Set up a timeline, set up a team, set up a system that will help you move toward your goal in a methodical fashion.

Then I developed strategies to maintain momentum and stay in action. According to one of Newton's laws of motion, an object in motion stays in motion. You must avoid inertia. I realized that achieving each small goal helped me stay in motion and that the process may not always proceed in a straight path. It is okay to change direction as many times as is necessary, but make sure to maintain the vision with the end goal in mind.

I have surrounded myself with people who have similar and bigger goals who will act as a support system to ensure accountability and prevent backsliding. My business has been created with winning teams in place, and the best is yet to come.

Author: Dr. Ndidiamaka Obadan

Dr. Ndidiamaka O. Obadan, fondly known as Dr. DD, is the CEO and founder of YoungerSelf MD, a medical practice aimed at preventing and treating adults with chronic medical conditions including diabetes, hypertension, and chronic kidney disease. She is board-certified in internal medicine, nephrology, and hypertension and has worked in the community setting as a hospitalist and in academics as an affiliate assistant professor.

Dr. Obadan lives with her husband and three children in Kennesaw, Georgia. She can be found on Instagram: @youngerself.md.

CHAPTER 24

PREPARATION CREATES **OPPORTUNITY**

D o you know anyone who sat back in their chair fiddling their thumbs and huge opportunities came to them by simply existing? I don't.

In residency, there were grand rounds and medical staff meetings. Despite my rigorous schedule, I would always attend because it's important to be in the room where people see your face. This led to me being the face of my residency program, and upon graduation, I was offered a job at my hospital. Not all of us were offered a contract.

I then prepared to be a media expert on TV, not knowing how, but knowing it would happen. In February 2017, entering my first job out of residency, I had a lawyer add an addendum to my contract stating that I could do all media. Although I did not get the opportunity to be on TV until November 2018, I was prepared.

Strong work ethic *now* helps you leverage for opportunities *later*. Once, I had a patient observe my tender care and how I took the time to simplify and explain complex medical jargon to her. Unbeknownst to me at the time, she was a producer for CNN/HLN with seventeen years of experience. She placed me on national live TV as a medical expert with no prior TV experience. She bet on me based on my care for her.

Another example—only one year into my career, I was asked to be the lead physician of a brand-new primary care center by the biggest hospital system in Georgia. Within eight months of opening that new practice, it was thriving. I leveraged that success to decrease from a five-day to a four-day work week.

Preparation is important to not only be ready for opportunity but also to create opportunity. Preparation is you in action, constantly working on yourself and your brand. It is reading books and listening to podcasts to acquire new skills. It is networking by being in rooms with people you emulate.

Opportunity comes through your network. Whether your access to the network is free or you have to pay for it, the information you gather is crucial. Networking connects you to people who can open doors that would otherwise have remained closed.

Why would someone help you through these doors? Because they are watching you in action. People want to help those who help themselves. They see your work ethic, your drive, your interactions with other people, and they then decide if they would enjoy working with you or if they would recommend you to others. When people know you will represent them well, they will bet on you because you make them look good.

However, do the right thing solely because it's the right thing to do. How you do the small things is how you do the big things. Your character and your reputation precedes you.

I'll give you some instances:

1. I am the founder of a networking group for female judges, attorneys, and physicians in Atlanta. My driver's license was suspended in 2020 (don't ask), but luckily an attorney in the group represented me pro bono to get the citation dropped. She felt glad to do this gratis (for free) because I gave her some medical advice a few months earlier.

2. I have realized that I don't have to be an expert in every subject to be successful. If you don't know the answer, the answer is in the room. For example, my house is a tornado. I have a close girlfriend who is a professional organizer, and she is helping me unpack and organize my home.

3. I am conventionally trained and family medicine board certified but also want to learn integrative functional medicine. I have endeared myself to one of the best integrative functional medicine physicians in Atlanta. We collaborate. I get to practice holistically on the job versus getting board certified first.

I knew I would go into private practice at some point in my career, but I expected to remain a hospital-employed physician until I had children and was strategically ready. But because of moral injury, which led to burnout, I left the hospital earlier than expected by opting out of a contract renewal. I realized I would rather be unemployed than working in corporate America disguised as medicine.

Because of my reputation, a colleague found out about my predicament and offered to become my business partner. She is helping me open up a private practice by fronting the administrative staff and money. I don't have to go through the mistakes that my partner already went through. She's taking a risk on me by investing her time, resources, and money. Preparation creates opportunity.

Being in action evolves your personal brand and network. Doing what is right always sets you up for success even if the reward is not in the place you do the good work. Your network will present the opportunities and open new doors. You have access to expertise that is not in your skillset through your network.

Through action, you may get immediate opportunities. Other times, it's delayed. You may not be presented with opportunities until you grow into the person ready for them, so always be in action. Always be preparing.

Now I am opening up my private practice with the help of my network, but I was preparing for this opportunity for years before it was presented. Today is the day to intentionally prepare yourself, because preparation creates opportunity!

Author: Dr. Barbara Joy Jones-Parks

Dr. Barbara Joy Jones is a board-certified family medicine physician with proficiency in osteopathic manipulative treatment. She is the chief medical officer of The Healthy Woman Primary Care. When she isn't doctoring, she can be found on live national TV as a medical expert contributor for CNN/HLN or on the runway as a professional model.

She lives in Norcross, Georgia with her husband, Lewis. You can follow her on Instagram: @TheModelDoc.

©Ron Witherspoon Photography

CHAPTER 25

CONSERVATIVE

Another Name for Afraid

" Ashti Loo" is a nickname derived from my middle and last name. It was my social media handle for many years, but I was making changes on every social media platform to scrub my legal name from the internet. My goal was complete anonymity, and to achieve this, my profiles became private and undiscoverable. La Toya Asha Luces, MD, her training and current place of employment, were the only traces of me that could be found.

I am a very private person, and I wanted to maintain a separation between my social life and my professional life as a physician. Even on my social media profiles, I rarely posted and secretly judged others who chose to expose themselves on the internet. They were attention seekers, and I was a conservative professional who enjoyed life but privately. My real friends knew how to identify me, and that was enough.

I made all of my old posts, from my pre-attending life, private. I made sure any comments that had my name were deleted, and I did several Google searches to identify areas where my legal name could be found, making sure the results related only to my medical practice. I carefully selected who I added as a Facebook friend or allowed to follow me on Instagram. I routinely went through my friend list, purging contacts—I was serious. I had a system that worked well for me and kept me grounded. When 2020 became too much to handle, I disabled all of my accounts easily, and it had no impact on my life.

As the pandemic raged, I, like many people, made a decision to make the most of my time and develop the business idea that had been sitting at the back of my mind. My business, a curated directory of Black-owned businesses and Black professionals who cater to the Black community, had nothing to do with medicine, and I didn't want to be directly associated with it.

I devised an elaborate, foolproof plan: I was going to create a false identity and only use my voice in marketing campaigns, if necessary. I even considered using a stand-in for appearances, all so that I could remain private and professional. I could continue being a physician, my business would magically grow on its own, and no one would ever know that I was behind it all. Genius!

Like most physicians, I did not have a business background and was unclear about where to begin. I was introduced to business coaching and decided that it would be a worthwhile investment to guide me along the uncharted waters of entrepreneurship.

Imagine my dismay when, very early in the program, I was told that my personal story was what was needed to grow my business. My genius plan was falling apart before my eyes. I just couldn't wrap my mind around the idea of speaking in public. There was an intake form for the coaching program that asked what was the biggest challenge I faced as an entrepreneur. I didn't list issues with finding legal counsel or figuring out my business model— I wrote about all the reasons I didn't think it was a good idea for me to be the face of my business.

It took several weeks before I realized that the narrative that I had created for myself, of this conservative physician, was a fallacy. In real life, I was actually quite the opposite. So if I wasn't actually conservative, then all that was left was that I was just afraid. Afraid of the comments and hate from strangers; afraid that my friends would think I was trying to cultivate a fake, reality TV persona; afraid that my patients and colleagues would think that I was unprofessional and that my business was completely inappropriate for a physician.

Once I made this realization, the barriers I had created for myself slowly started to break down. The first major step was changing my social media handle to my actual name. I'll be honest, I used my married name instead of my maiden name, which is how I am known as a physician. I was still holding back a bit, but it was progress!

My next steps were making my social media profiles public and starting a YouTube channel. I recorded my first video, telling the story of why I created the business, and the response was so overwhelmingly positive that it blew my mind. I then started an interview series, where I interviewed the CEOs of businesses that would be listed in my directory. This series was so popular that I had a waiting list for interviews.

I also began doing weekly Facebook and Instagram lives. These started off very short and were always preceded by nausea, tachycardia, and diaphoresis, but at least I was showing up. With time, I became much more comfortable doing them and even started asking the viewers to join me live, and many did. I was invited to do live and prerecorded interviews, and I became the face of my brand.

Every time I told my story, I made another connection, gained another follower, and collected another email address. People could now relate directly to me and the instant respect gained from the fact that I was a physician could not be ignored. As I became more comfortable, I started infusing more of my personality into my marketing. The creative, funny, and social me was allowed to come out, and this impressive human emerged. I had finally started to own and celebrate every part of me, and as I did, more doors opened, as people were equally intrigued and impressed that with all I had already achieved, I was now adding the title of entrepreneur.

It seemed as though I had become a new person, but I actually fully embraced the whole individual that I was all along. I am Dr. Toya: physician, prodigy, mother, wife, daughter, sister, diver, bungee jumper, world traveler, and CEO.

Still a little private but no longer afraid.

Author: Dr. La Toya Luces-Sampson

Dr. La Toya Luces-Sampson, also known as Dr. Toya, is a wife, mother, board-certified OB/GYN, and entrepreneur. She is the founder and CEO of Buy Default, a curated directory of Black-owned businesses and Black professionals who cater to the Black community. She is also the CEO of Amina OB/GYN Consultants, a locum tenens company offering hospital-based OB/GYN services in the state of California.

Dr. Toya is passionate about service to her community and patients and uses entrepreneurship to serve them both in her own way and on her own terms. Follow her on Instagram: @buy_default.

CHAPTER 26

DON'T LET FEAR SLAM THE DOOR ON YOUR **DREAMS**!

What day is it? Stop looking at me, please! This is what went through my head as I sat, mute, in a medical school lecture when asked to state the day of the week. I was painfully introverted.

Because of this and because I lacked confidence in my ability to exercise authority, I, for way too long, quietly and obediently followed what others decided was my appropriate path. Let me share my story and save you time, money, and frustration!

For as long as I could remember, extreme introversion and timid obedience were all I knew. In school, written tests were my friend. If I had to do a presentation, I got it done but anxiously. In college, my Russian language professor refused to believe I was not a native Russian speaker—that's how good my Russian was—but I dreaded being called on to read aloud. When my fear came true, I raced through the text as fast as possible just to be done.

In medical school, when I started seeing patients, I suppressed my fears by pretending I was an actor playing the role of a doctor. In ophthalmology residency, during morning report, another resident said she heard me whispering all the answers, and I should raise my hand to respond. She did not realize the minute everyone looked my way, I would barely be able to state my name. Upon entering private practice as a refractive surgeon and corneal and external disease specialist, I still struggled with activities such as making phone calls.

Soon after training, I got married, settled into a job working six days a week, and got pregnant. Due to placenta previa, I started bleeding around twenty-nine weeks and was admitted to the hospital on complete bed rest for about a month. At thirty-four weeks, my daughter was born preterm but healthy. Once able, I returned to practice part time as an independent contractor.

My daughter was remarkably intelligent and meeting her milestones. Despite normal vision, however, she avoided making eye contact. When severe anxiety interfered with her toilet training, I took her to a neurodevelopmental pediatrician. She was diagnosed with autism. She was also diagnosed with what that veteran doctor described as the worst case of anxiety he had seen in someone her age.

Around the same time, I had my second daughter. She was colicky. My plate was full.

I continued working part time. It seemed reasonable, given everything. I had a lot to take care of at home, and most of the energy our family had left over was dedicated to decisions involving my husband's career as a busy attorney at a large firm. Any discussion of my starting or buying a practice was met with discouragement and lack of faith.

My marriage suffered and ultimately did not survive. For multiple reasons, most importantly great schools, my daughters and I moved to the suburbs, forty-five minutes from their father and the only home they knew. It was an adjustment but best for everyone.

Time marched on. My younger daughter became serious about dance, and my older daughter was still requiring a one-on-one paraprofessional in high school. Despite that, they were both growing older and more independent. I increased my hours at work.

Unfortunately, work as an independent contractor provides no option for practice ownership. Years prior, when I had considered starting my own practice, I lacked not only the necessary support but also the self-confidence needed to take charge as a boss and practice owner. Now I needed to advance my career so I could care for my daughters and prepare financially for our future.

For many years, my inner drive for personal growth had inspired reflection. Eventually, that led to the realization that fear was no excuse! The time to forge my own path had come!

Soon after arriving at that understanding, while scrolling online, I saw an announcement for a free online summit for physicians interested in maintaining multiple income streams. An interview from that summit featured a doctor, Nneka Unachukwu (Dr. Una). She had started her own successful practice and, subsequently, a business school to teach other doctors to do the same. She was brilliant, effervescent!

In medical school, no one taught us to start and run practices. We were supposed to learn the science and patient care and let others take care of the rest. That they did, and now doctors and patients alike suffer! No more! Now it was up to me!

I did more research but knew if I was serious about opening my practice, I could use guidance and inspiration. Dr. Una's business school would provide both, as well as a community of like-minded physicians with whom to share questions, concerns, and support. It was exactly what I needed.

In June 2021, I joined. The direction, community, and encouragement fostered the conviction I needed to start. Since then, I have incorporated my business and found an attorney and an accountant. I designed a logo and started my business Facebook page on which I post regularly. I created a VIP waitlist for my practice as well as a lead magnet for my Facebook page. Then I researched and interviewed for, but have not yet hired, a virtual assistant.

To further build my brand, I became a village sponsor, led webinars with local senior groups, went on multiple podcasts, and started a Facebook live series, Everything about Eyes. Along with my attorney, I negotiated and signed lease and practice management agreements. I wrote a business projection to secure a loan, chose and ordered equipment, and found a contractor to configure the space. As I write this, my website is in progress. I have insurance contracts in place, have applied for hospital staff privileges, and have chosen an electronic health records system.

It's coming together! ReEnvision Eye Care will open soon.

Save yourself time. We all fear imperfection, the unknown. Strive for perfection, but in entrepreneurship, excellence is fantastic! As Roy T. Bennett said, "Don't be pushed around by the fears in your mind. Be led by the dreams in your heart!" Write *your* story now. Do it...scared. Start. Confidence will follow.

Author: Dr. Kristi L. Kozlov, FAAO

Kristi Kozlov, MD, is a board-certified ophthalmologist and fellowship-trained corneal specialist. She is Founder and CEO of ReEnvision Eye Care, where she helps maintain and restore patients' sight so they can live their best lives. She has served as a guest on multiple podcasts, educating the public on ocular health.

Dr. Kozlov lives in Buffalo Grove, Illinois with her two daughters. She loves international travel and learning about other cultures and languages. You can follow her on Facebook at ReEnvision Eye Care.

CHAPTER 27

GET OUT OF YOUR HEAD AND INTO A **COMMUNITY**

I t took me only ten days to launch two online businesses, yet it took me six years of *thinking* about starting a business before actually getting it done.

Ten days for the state to process my LLC application, and concurrently, one week of working with a designer to build my website. A couple of hours to set up malpractice insurance, a video conferencing platform, and payment processor, and I was officially in business.

But not before I had spent six long years of trying to start my business alone, solitarily researching and planning a dream that year after year I failed to bring to life.

I do not regret my long and winding path to entrepreneurship because I have learned so much and grown tremendously along the way. But I do wish to help any super introverted and fiercely self-reliant doctors like me save valuable time and avoid unnecessary pain by sharing one of my favorite lessons learned: the key to starting a business, and the best part of the journey, is getting out of your head and connecting with a community of people.

My first job out of residency was as the sole psychiatrist for a multidisciplinary community mental health team. We drove across rural North Carolina to bring psychiatric services to the homes of patients. Without such care, our vulnerable population would spend their entire lives in hospitals and jails due the severity of their mental illnesses. I loved my challenging and endearing patients. I also felt honored to work alongside many warm and capable clinicians.

But problems with the administrative and nonclinical aspects of the job slowly chipped away at my career satisfaction. For the first time, I started to feel like a cog in a corporate wheel, instead of a valued member of a healthcare team. Nonclinicians and insurance companies questioned my clinical decisions and wielded unearned influence over patient care. I spent an inordinate amount of time dealing with prior authorizations and fighting to get my patients the medications they needed. I soon realized that practicing medicine like this was not going to lead to the fulfilled and happy life I had envisioned when I first decided to become a doctor.

Listening to podcasts by women entrepreneurs sparked the idea that there was more to life than working for someone else and playing by their rules. I came to believe that a life of freedom, purpose, impact, and fulfillment were possible and that starting my own business might be the way.

I spent all of my free time dreaming up new business ideas. I had notepads full of research and plans. Yet, years went by, and I was no closer to having a business. There was something holding me back, but I was not quite sure what it was.

Over the years post residency, I practiced in various settings and noticed that things in medicine seemed to be quickly devolving from mildly frustrating to downright intolerable for many. Physician turnover was extremely high at my job. I saw at least seven physicians in my little department alone come and go in a year, a reflection of how untenable the work conditions had become. We all felt on edge and stressed out due to the lack of support from leadership and staff. I saw some of my colleagues fired without a clear explanation. I personally knew doctors who were furloughed in the middle of the COVID-19 pandemic, despite patient care needs being at an all-time high. I was kicked out of my office and relocated to a windowless cubicle in the bowels of the hospital to make space for an administrator.

When our concerns about work conditions fell on deaf ears, drowned out by the indifference of leadership who did nothing to help, I knew I needed to make a change. The clear unsustainability of working in corporate medicine, coupled with the painful realization that I may have avoided this situation had I started my business years ago as planned, was the push I needed to finally seek coaching.

When I joined EntreMD, the lightbulb went off and I saw the piece I had been missing for years was community. As an introvert and independent spirit, I had underestimated how much I needed to lean on other people. And deep down, I was afraid of putting myself out there. But in EntreMD, I felt right at home.

Through Dr. Una's amazing coaching and the support of like-minded physicians in our community, I went from having a muddled tangle of half-baked ideas to a clear business model through which I now create the impact I had envisioned. All the solo research and daydreaming in the world could not have brought me such clarity and forward action. But community and coaching did.

My mindset shifted from avoiding discomfort to seeing the value in daring my fears and putting myself out there so I could grow. I became a speaker, showing up on podcasts, Facebook lives, and even at the EntreMD Business Expo in front of hundreds of doctors. I turned my blog into a powerful business asset, and I am now adding published author to my list of wins through my contribution to this book.

The generosity and warmth of the physicians in EntreMD inspired me to dedicate my business to serving women in medicine. I now have not one but two businesses: a niche psychiatry and psychotherapy practice and a coaching program, both geared to women physicians who suffer from undiagnosed mental illness and suicide rates that are 130 percent higher than the general population.

I am finally creating the impact and life I started dreaming of years ago. And more importantly, because of community, I have authentic connections and real-life friendships that have enriched my life more than I ever imagined.

Author: Dr. Jeannie Collins Lawrence

Dr. Jeannie Lawrence is a board-certified psychiatrist, psycho-therapist, and coach who is passionate about empowering women physicians to flourish, both inside and out. She is the CEO of two companies dedicated to this mission: her private clinical practice specializes in mental health for women physicians. Her coaching practice helps women in medicine optimize their well-being while achieving their most audacious dreams.

Dr. Lawrence has authored dozens of articles and is a sought-after speaker and expert. She has been featured on the local news and numerous podcasts and has been invited to speak on national stages.

She lives in North Carolina with her husband, Bashan. Follow her on Instagram: @dr.jeannielawrencemd.

CHAPTER 28

BIG ENTREPRENEURIAL DREAMS CAN COME IN **MICRO** FORMS

Do you suffer from having "I love and want to do it all" syndrome? Then my story may be familiar to you…

On a day that resembled so many before, I arrived late to the program directors' meeting after being delayed at the clinic. While in the meeting, I received a text from my husband. He wasn't going to be able to pick up one of our two kids. Pickup duties were typically split between us, so I was going to have to leave the meeting early in order to pick up both kids on time.

During the meeting, I was more distracted than usual—I was thinking about my to-do list for the evening after the kids were in bed. I also kept reflecting on business ideas that had been coming to mind.

As a multi-passionate person, I suffer from having "I love and want to do it all" syndrome. I loved being a physician mom in an academic setting, but I also had entrepreneurial desires to create a business that added value to the community. Furthermore, I wanted to have work-life integration that allowed time for self-care and time for my family.

I used to believe that all entrepreneurial endeavors existed in an intimidating black box that required an impossible undertaking for me as a physician and mother of young children. With everything I already had on my plate, my internal monologue was rife with thoughts that would keep me from taking action. Thoughts such as, *In order to be successful, I will need to run myself into the ground*; *I'll have to quit my job to be an entrepreneur*; and *If it's not a huge business, then it's a failure... There's no point in even trying*.

In my desire to be an entrepreneur, I wanted to have something that was my own, where I could practice my way on my terms. I wanted something small and manageable, profitable, and could fit within my career and family. It was also important that it wouldn't take over all of my time and had growth potential. However, the growth had to happen at a pace that I could handle.

It was almost as if I was searching for a paradoxical entity. The question remained: Did such a thing exist, and how in the world was I going to make this happen?

Through accessing online communities, coaching, and various resources, a few things became apparent: I wasn't crazy to dare to dream for something that was nontraditional, and in fact, there were people in medicine who had done what I desired and were thriving. I discovered that having a big dream involving entrepreneurship does not have to mean owning a large, life-consuming business. Alternative forms of dreaming big can entail an entrepreneurial life that fits into the crevices of your life based on the stage and season you are in. You can be a successful entrepreneur with the ultimate goal of creating a business that suits your desired work-life integration framework, no matter what your life looks like.

I discovered that the manifestation of my vision and the cure for my "I love and want to do it all" syndrome was going to be in the form of a part-time micropractice. A micropractice is a practice where the overarching goal is a practice with low overhead and little to no staff outside of the owner. You can have a full-time micropractice or part-time model that opens a few days a week. My micropractice business model was to open a part-time practice that best fit into my schedule. From this vision, Vivant Medical Services, PLLC was born.

Along my journey, there were valuable lessons to learn and myths that I had to dispel. "Small" didn't mean not profitable, "small" didn't mean I wasn't dreaming big, and "small" didn't mean it wasn't going to take some sacrifice and hard work.

In doing the work to create a professional and personal life on my terms, there were difficult decisions and sacrifices needing to be made. For example, I was going to have to significantly scale back the time that I could devote to certain elements of my academic career. My family was also going to need to relocate due to family reasons, leaving the comforts of the community and colleagues that I had grown to adore. My pursuit of this business was going to happen in an environment where I had no network or connections within the medical community. For me, this journey was going to require huge changes that were uncomfortable, scary, and full of uncertainties.

However, within six months of registering the business and utilizing a strategic business framework, I had a location, contracts secured to provide clinical services, and a set launch date. It was astonishing to reflect on the transition of going from an idea to reality once I shifted my mindset about entrepreneurship. The power of having coaches, business mentors, and a supportive community of like-minded physicians and entrepreneurs were key in navigating the process and propelling me forward.

What I learned through the experience was that sometimes a vision takes a hold of you before there is a tangible example. This is the beauty of entrepreneurship; I saw what I wanted to create but didn't have a blueprint for how to get from A to Z. The journey has been filled with highs, lows, doubts, rewards, challenges, and everything in between. Nonetheless, pursuing my business reinforced my belief that if you can see it and believe it, then you can manifest and create it, even if you do not have all of the answers ahead of time.

The greatest reward is not just the business but is, in fact, the person that you become during the process. In evolving as a person, your dreams and what you see as possible evolve as well. I believe this is best said in one of my favorite quotes by Marissa Mayer: "If you push through that feeling of being scared, that feeling of taking risk, really amazing things can happen."

Author: Dr. Olabisi Badmus

Dr. Olabisi Badmus (Dr. Bisi) is a double board-certified physician specializing in preventive medicine/public health and occupational medicine. She is the owner and CEO of Vivant Medical Services and holds faculty appointments at multiple academic institutions. Using her knowledge and passion for health equity, career-life integration, and workforce wellness, she consults and speaks on these topics and also serves as a resource to help other physicians interested in starting a micropractice.

Dr. Bisi resides in Charlotte, North Carolina with her husband and two kids. You can follow her on Instagram: @DrBisi_MD.

178 · SECTION II: **STARTUPS**

CHAPTER 29

ENTREPRENEURSHIP IS AN ACT OF **RESISTANCE**

Here are some facts that really disturb me: physicians experience burnout and suicide at dramatically higher rates than the general population. Women physicians experience these things, plus divorce and early retirement, at dramatically higher rates than men physicians do.

I remember when I first heard that data, and I wasn't surprised one bit. I had seen the statistics play out in my own life and in the lives of my friends.

In the fall of 2015, the weight of all the expectations I had been trying to meet became more than I could bear. The messages I had internalized about what it means to be a good mother, a good doctor, a good wife, a good person required more than any human could possibly be or do. I started wishing I would get sick or injured just so I could justify some time alone without the hustle for worthiness. As things got worse, I started having death fantasies. My brutal self-talk, born of those unrealistic expectations, kept me from seeing that it was the expectations themselves, not me, that were the problem.

Thankfully, I got the help I needed from a therapist and an amazing group of family and friends who helped me find myself again. I have spent the years since working hard to understand the causes and solutions to physician burnout, especially for women. First, this was for my own benefit and, later, to help others struggling with the same problems.

It's a tragedy for physicians to live their lives resigned to dissatisfaction and burnout. I want us all to flourish. But for that to happen, we must address the things that keep us from flourishing.

What does all that have to do with entrepreneurship? There are essential skills for living a flourishing life, and many of them can be honed through the process of becoming an entrepreneur. Martin Seligman, the world's foremost researcher on human flourishing, has found that the factor contributing most to a person's life satisfaction is recognizing and then developing their unique strengths in service of a purpose larger than themselves. Developing and using your strengths requires some level of autonomy, but lack of autonomy has become a major problem for physicians. It's one of the biggest contributors to burnout. There is no greater cure for this than to start your own business.

I don't mean that you have to leave your clinical practice; starting small can bring big benefits. For me, starting the *Women Physicians Flourish* podcast and developing a group course gave me a much needed injection of autonomy. These have been more than just side projects—they've changed my perspective on the rest of my work. Because of the work I did to bring these projects to fruition, I feel more capable. I am more interested and involved in the business aspects of my practice, where I used to defer that to someone else. I feel more freedom, even though my clinical practice is the same.

Another overlap between the skills of flourishing and entre-preneurship is the courage and vulnerability required to dream of something new and bring it to life. Starting a business is risky and can draw criticism. Most women in America are conditioned to avoid criticism, to suppress their own desires and focus on fulfilling the desires of others, to stay in supportive roles. Even women physicians, with our advanced education, high income potential, and social status are subject to this conditioning. Too many of us stay quiet and small.

My own inner critics kept me tied up for decades. Afraid of being different, afraid of what it meant if I wasn't perfect. Afraid of the double binds: too big, too small; too loud, too quiet; too bossy, too passive. Better to just stay invisible.

Ultimately, I had to make a choice: perfection and conformity, or joy and fulfillment. They can't coexist. I chose joy and fulfillment, and even though it's sometimes scary, I've never regretted it. I've chosen to listen to my own voice and to be discerning about whose criticism actually matters.

Physicians have had increasing levels of burnout and decreas-ing career satisfaction for decades. For many of us, large companies have bought out our practices, and insurance companies have power over the nuances of patient care. We stand up against a wall of corporations and regulations that put profits over people and devalue our experience as clinicians.

Women physicians have even more barriers to flourishing—we earn less money, are disproportionately underrepresented in leadership, and have a harder time getting promotions despite equivalent experience to our male counterparts. Women physicians do eight and a half hours a week more unpaid household and caregiving work than men physicians do and on average have narrower, less influential networks.

None of these things are going to fix themselves. Are you okay with these issues staying the same, or getting worse, as their trajectories suggest?

The title of my chapter mentions resistance. Here's where that comes in: imagine what the world could look like in ten years if we all begin to exercise the power we have to resist and change the harmful systems in which we live and practice, while taking loving care of ourselves. One excellent way to start is by creating and growing a business that allows you to bring your best qualities into the world. A business that not only helps you feel more freedom but that innovates and inspires, breathes life back into you, and gives you energy to bring creative solutions to the problems we face. You deserve to be happy and fulfilled, and the world is better when the best of you is fully expressed.

It may seem like pie in the sky, trying to end burnout and change the healthcare system, but after this year in the EntreMD

Business School, I'm convinced it's possible. I have seen up close the momentum and the massive change effected by my colleagues in just six months. I've changed in ways I never expected because of this amazing community.

We are all regular folks, like you, and we're just getting started. Come join us.

Author: Dr. Rebecca W. Lauderdale

Dr. Lauderdale is a board-certified internal medicine specialist who practices primary care for medically complex adults in south Mississippi. Her podcast and public speaking business, *Women Physicians Flourish*, was born from her own experience of burnout and subsequent study of human flourishing. Dr. Lauderdale has appeared on podcasts such as *This Osteopathic Life* and *Imposter to Unstoppable*, has led workshops for early-career physicians, and has spoken at regional conferences on the subject of physician flourishing.

She lives in Hattiesburg, Mississippi with her husband, three children, three dogs, and a cat. You can follow her on Instagram: @Dr.Lauderdale.

CHAPTER 30

CREATING MY
DREAM JOB

What do you do when your dream job is not compatible with your well-being?

My parents were both immigrants, raised to pursue the American dream, which in part meant getting the "dream job." Growing up, I attributed our comfortable lifestyle and happiness to my parents' success in their chosen professions. I wanted to follow their example, so I decided to become a physician and eventually found my dream specialty of urology.

Once I decided to become a urologist, I began to plan for my career after training. I was keenly aware of the health disparities that plague Black Americans and wanted a career that would significantly impact as many people as possible. I learned that minority communities experienced better health outcomes when cared for by racially and ethnically similar physicians. I also learned that minority physicians are more likely to serve minority and underserved patients. With this in mind, I decided my goal would be to recruit and train minority physicians to care for the larger community. I realized that becoming an academic urologist was my dream job.

With my goals set, I entered residency full of hope and purpose. Then reality struck. Unfortunately, one of the reasons so few minorities go into academic medicine is the microaggressions and racial bias we experience in the medical education system.

Early on, I was told I was a disappointment compared to other residents, I was not a team player, I was lazy, and I would not make a good academic urologist. I internalized these messages, and by the time I neared the end of training, I'd gone from a confident, extroverted person to someone who cried most days and avoided other physicians. I no longer had confidence in my abilities and could not imagine mentoring anyone. I decided to go into private practice because I could not thrive in the toxic academic environment I had come to know.

Then the COVID-19 pandemic hit, and with it came a shift in my mindset. It reminded me that life is short, and I wanted to build a career aligned with my goals. I had been trying to live inside the boundaries created by an environment, a system, where I could not thrive. With this change in mindset, I began to examine the limiting beliefs I held: (1) I have to go into academic medicine to recruit and mentor minority trainees, and (2) my impact in urology is dependent on me becoming an academic faculty member.

The pandemic also brought new opportunities—it forced residency programs to make all interviews virtual for the upcoming application season. As a result, multiple Black medical students began to seek advice from me on how to successfully match into a urology residency with these changes. With the help of other minority urology trainees, I organized a webinar to address these topics, featuring academic urologists who answered the students' questions. Next, I created a virtual urology interest group to support the urology applicants and mentor minority medical students in earlier years of study.

I began to envision a three-tiered mentorship model that would support Black urologists from medical school, through training, and for the rest of their careers. After nearly eleven years of medical education, I had many ideas on what support was needed based on the challenges I'd faced. I started reaching out to urologists around the country to share my vision. I found people were excited about my ideas and wanted to work with me. They also introduced me to others in their network who could help me achieve my goal.

These conversations helped clarify what I was creating: a system dedicated to supporting and promoting Black urologists. As I learned more about the state of diversity in urology, I learned that fewer than 300 urologists in the United States are Black, which amounts to 2 percent of the workforce. Furthermore, only around 4 percent of urologists are Hispanic. My research helped clarify why I wanted to create this system: to counteract the disparities in medical education and increase the recruitment and retention of minority urologists. Once I had my what and why, I realized that building a business around this new system would be my how. I then founded my nonprofit organization and pipeline program, Urology Unbound.

As exciting as this was, starting a nonprofit brought on a host of new challenges that came with new limiting beliefs: I only knew how to practice medicine. I had no clue how to run a business. I did not like or understand social media, so how could I advertise the pipeline program and recruit enough minority students to make a difference? Plus, I was about to start my first job in private practice, so how could I possibly do both?

Thankfully, around this time, a friend told me about *The EntreMD Podcast*. It took only a few episodes to convince me that I needed to join the EntreMD Business School (EBS), where I'm learning the skills needed to grow my business and to thrive.

Since starting Urology Unbound, my life and career have entirely changed. I've had the opportunity to speak at multiple national conferences and have published various manuscripts with students in my pipeline program and colleagues in my expanded network. I've organized successful programs for my trainees to provide the support I wish I had when I was in training. The American Urological Association even awarded me the 2021 Young Urologist of the Year to recognize my efforts. All of this during my first year out of training as a private practice urologist!

Most importantly, thirty-two students in my pipeline program matched into urology in 2021, representing 9 percent of their resident class! A residency chairman once remarked that I had achieved more in one year than most academicians do in their first five years out of training. When I started to protest the compliment, she told me that I was an academic urologist in no uncertain terms.

Through business coaching and networking with my classmates in EBS, I'm conquering my imposter syndrome and learning the skills that have already transformed my career and life. Through entrepreneurship, I've proven I don't need to give up on my dream job because I have the tools to build it myself.

Author: Dr. Shenelle Wilson

Dr. Shenelle Wilson is a fellowship-trained urologist and owner of the Metro Atlanta Urology and Pelvic Health Center. She's also the CEO of Urology Unbound, a nonprofit dedicated to increasing diversity in urology. Dr. Wilson has spoken extensively about diversity in the physician workforce on multiple platforms and was awarded the 2021 American Urological Association Young Urologist of the Year for the Southeast section for her work.

Dr. Wilson lives near her family in Atlanta, Georgia with her seventeen-year-old toy poodle. You can find out more about her work on Instagram: @shenellewilsonmd.

CHAPTER 31

SUNGLASSES AND
VISIONS

Eighteen years ago, I moved from India to sunny Florida. I was an ambitious twenty-something-year-old, a fresh medical graduate with a vision.

I remember my very first day out sightseeing, after having arrived a couple of days before. I wanted to go see the local major hospital—that's how passionate I was about my career in medicine. So off we went, my husband and I, to Jackson Memorial Hospital in Miami. I was excited and felt very much at home. I introduced myself and asked to go to the department of pediatrics.

I just wanted to see the department, but I ended up at the residency program's office instead—probably because I looked like a student. The secretary was very welcoming. She informed me that they had an observership program for overseas students and that I was welcome to apply. She asked me when I would be ready to join. I replied, "Right now!" Amused, she handed me the application form. As I exited the building to meet with my husband who was waiting outside, the blaring Miami sun hit my eye. I didn't have a pair of sunglasses with me at that time, so I had to squint as I walked around the place.

You see, I was never that much into sunglasses. I thought they made people look flashy, and I certainly did not have the personality that loved to stand out in a crowd. Well, I wasn't thinking of the big picture. By trying to be modest, I was missing out on an essential accessory that could be protective to my eyes.

I subsequently joined the observership program and stayed on for three months. During this time, I built relationships and made great first impressions. I eventually did my residency in pediatrics at this very same program and started my career as a pediatrician. Pediatrics was my passion, and I was a bright-eyed new residency graduate with great ideas and an abundance of zeal. I was determined to give it my best.

But the next ten years were no easy ride. I certainly had my share of ups and downs and thankfully survived them all. Now as I look back, though I never realized it at that time, those dips came when I was trying to stick to my comfort zone, somewhat oblivious to the changes happening in my profession.

The healthcare system, like anything else, was not meant to stay the same forever. The world of corporate medicine reared its ugly head and progressively penetrated into the core of the system, gearing it more toward maximization of profit rather than quality healthcare. What started as a calling felt like a routine day-to-day job, where I was trying to meet expectations. Although I was making decisions for my patients, I certainly was not in control of my environment. And that affected my ability to do the best I could as a physician. The once bright spark in my eyes was slowly starting to dim. And I realized I was not alone. There were dissatisfied patients and equally dissatisfied doctors everywhere.

But we doctors are innovators and warriors—we just don't realize it. Well, at least, most of us don't. Since staying in my comfort zone was not the answer, I started looking around and saw my fellow physicians adapting to change in many different ways. I was inspired. Just by starting to network with other physicians, I realized that I could change too. I was meant for more, and it was time to take things in stride.

And then came 2020, giving us all a jolt from the blue. Rightfully called the year of clarity in hindsight, physicians got a much-needed wake-up call. I joined the EntreMD Business School that very year in a quest to learn about physician entrepreneurship and starting a practice. Well, that was the whole turning point. In less than a year, I took the leap of faith and WonderKidz Pediatrics LLC was launched.

I am now the CEO of my own space with a bigger vision. Building a practice from scratch is a fascinating experience in itself, but the greatest reward is that you also build yourself up, growing alongside the practice. It took me all these years to realize that I was an expert in my field and could do a lot besides seeing patients within the four walls of my office. Healthcare, as it was a decade or two back, had become a thing of the past, and it was time to write our own stories in keeping with the changing times.

Information technology has given way to a lot of mis- and disinformation, and our patients need to hear from us first. As physicians, our voice is powerful, and it is only fair to our patients that we give them the right information before they get something from a wrong source. The old me would never have thought about being a guest speaker at a local event, but I am not hesitant to speak in public anymore. My very first blog saw the light of the day soon after I started my business, and I learned to navigate social media and present myself to the world as the expert that I always was.

So here I was, working on my business and my YouTube channel on health and wellness for children. I finally felt a sense of purpose and fulfillment in what I did. By reliving my life with a whole new perspective, I discovered a happiness that I didn't know I had subdued with my own limiting beliefs. My strength was all that I needed to take back my calling and live the life that I always wanted.

There is a whole new world beyond your horizon. So I dare you, dear reader, to break out of the box and explore the world without limitations.

And yes, I am into fancy sunglasses these days!

Author: Dr. Violina Bhattacharyya, FAAP

Dr. Violina Bhattacharyya is a board-certified pediatrician practicing in Hollywood, Florida. She is the founder and CEO of Wonderkidz Pediatrics, which was started with a mission to help children with behavioral health concerns at the primary care level. With a goal of educating the community on child health and wellness, she has been featured on podcasts and is a regular blog contributor at Broward Mom Collective, a local moms group.

Dr. Bhattacharyya resides in South Florida with her husband and two children. You can follow her on Instagram: @wonder kidzpediatrics.

CHAPTER 32

WHY START A **NEW** BUSINESS IN YOUR SIXTIES

Why would anyone start a new business at age sixty-four? Especially a physician who had been in practice for over thirty years, loved working with patients, and was close to what is considered retirement age?

Because I love working with people.

I practiced gynecology in Georgia for almost thirty years and left my practice when my husband, Steve, and I relocated to the Florida Panhandle for a fabulous position that we could not pass up. I did not want to leave my beloved patients, friends, and community, but I could not live without my husband anymore. He had already been commuting long distances to work for over twelve years, while waiting for a local opportunity to open up. I gained forty-five pounds during the time that he worked away from home. Additionally, I was burned out dealing with the day-to-day administrative burden of running a medical office and was ready to take a break. So I relocated with him.

Although the loneliness of living in a new community was predictable, it was still depressing. My gym workouts helped me maintain my sanity. I became a plant-centered eater after reading *The China Study* and lost twenty-five of the forty-five pounds gained. Once we settled into our new home, I applied for a Florida medical license and was offered a gynecology position in a local medical group. Finally!

In the fall of 2019, in the same week that my license was approved, I fell while hiking and tore 100 percent of my right rotator cuff tendons, requiring surgery and a lengthy rehabilitation. It was tedious and painful, but I experienced many blessings from my time in rehab. A couple of those blessings included having my work contract canceled and lots of time to read!

Three monumental things happened to me during the time I spent in rehab that changed my life:

1. I discovered the newly organized medical specialty called lifestyle medicine and became board certified. This would become my life's work. How does one describe the passion for something that sets your heart on fire?

2. I discovered the American Telemedicine Association at their annual conference and realized how powerful it would be for patients to receive care in the privacy of their homes.

3. I started listening to podcasts and fell in love with Dr. Una and EntreMD. I listened to every episode and could not wait for the next one. She helped me see that starting a new business was realistic and logical, no matter my age.

However, there were all kinds of problems to solve if I wanted to start a new medical practice:

- It was too expensive to start a brick-and-mortar solo practice in a city where I was unknown.
- Telemedicine was not accepted practice in 2019; insurance companies did not reimburse for it; and HIPAA-compliant platforms were difficult to come by.
- Most people were not familiar with, or comfortable with, how to access remote care.
- I didn't have a clue how to talk to people through a webcam, let alone an iPhone.
- The unknown and foreign world of navigating the new age of social media, including marketing. (Well, it was new to me! I was a teen in the 1970s.)
- The legalities of running an online business and medical practice.
- How to gain trust in a community where I was unknown.
- My totally incapacitating, paralyzing fear of public speaking, which I saw as the only avenue to developing trust and relationships in my new community.

All of this created quite the emotional stew for me. Every day my mind's negative voices would chant, "You can't do this," "Why do you want to do this?" "You will *never* be able to speak in front of a group; you are so afraid," "You are crazy," and "You are too old."

Amid these thoughts was the ever-present drumbeat of the critical mission to practice lifestyle medicine, which included helping as many people as possible to prevent, arrest, and potentially reverse their chronic diseases. The fact that 80 percent of chronic diseases in our country are due to lifestyle choices (the standard American diet, lack of sleep, stress, lack of movement, alcohol, drug, and tobacco use) is staggering. Imagine our country, our friends, and loved ones with 80 percent less suffering, pain, disease, and early deaths.

The mission for me remains crystal clear, and it continues to drive me to find solutions to the many problems that exist in developing this practice, including public speaking. The mission is much more important and much larger than my personal problems.

Joining Dr. Una's EntreMD Business School was the best investment in helping me develop and move toward success in my business. Listening to Dr. Una's podcasts, participating in the live coaching, being surrounded with honest, supportive, and loving fellow physician entrepreneurs, and working the business school curriculum was completely transformative for me.

It was a very slow process, but it changed my thinking nevertheless. The negative thoughts dissipated over time, and the positive mantras dominated my thinking as a constant happy newsfeed. "Yes, I can do this," "This is exciting," "Age will not define me,"

"I have faith that it will work." "I can be a public speaker and dominate the stage. The message is much too *critical* to sit at home in silence."

It has taken a couple of years to develop my practice model, but I am thrilled to say we will open for business soon. This practice is unique in that one eight-week course will provide interactive group coaching, support, and instruction in all six pillars of lifestyle medicine delivered via a telemedicine platform. People will be able to access us in the privacy of their homes.

I have the deepest gratitude for Dr. Una and the EntreMD Business School. It is her faith, expertise, tenacity, and love for fellow physicians that has inspired me to create this new entrepreneurial life! Dr. Una, you are a treasure. Thanks a million!

Author: Dr. Erin Mayfield

Dr. Erin Mayfield is board certified in OB/GYN and lifestyle medicine and earned her CHEF Coaching certification through Harvard University. After a thirty-plus-year career as an OB/GYN, she developed a new lifestyle medicine practice called Lifestyle Medicine Wellness and Recovery, LLC.

Dr. Mayfield is passionate about helping people understand the evidence-based science behind whole plant food nutrition and the potential for people to prevent, arrest, and potentially reverse chronic diseases. She has a YouTube channel showcasing fellow docs cooking healthy plant-based meals, has been a guest on numerous podcasts, is a speaker, and hosts the only Walk with a Doc chapter in the Florida Panhandle.

Dr. Mayfield is grateful for the full support of her husband, Steve, and their three sweet, loving canines! Find her on Instagram: @lifestylemedwellnessrecovery.

CHAPTER 33

DO IT WRONG, THEN DO IT AGAIN ... **BETTER**

I f I could encourage my younger self from just eighteen months ago, the advice to "Do it wrong" would likely be met with skepticism. My current vantage point of a future full of tangible dreams and financial freedom was not imaginable to the primary care doctor trapped in a nine-to-five, committed to serving the inner-city community of New York, settling for a below-average salary, hoping to "make a difference" through self-sacrifice and long suffering. At the height of the pandemic in June 2020, I could be found in my prayer corner tearfully begging for change but unsure of the path toward change.

I had desired a change that would bring me freedom from the nine-to-five. A freedom to allow me to pursue hobbies and passion projects. A flexibility that would allow regular travel for medical mission trips. And freedom to write stories of hard-learned lessons to be shared with the next generation.

This was a change I had dreamed of for years, and suddenly it was knocking at the door in the form of an old friend.

A chiropractor friend approached me with a request. The neurologist who normally saw patients once a week at her office was retiring and moving out of state, which left her office with an opening. With thirty years of experience under her belt, she had full knowledge of the trade. She generously offered to share her staff and office equipment with me.

So my private practice was born.

I established Wellspring Health, a micropractice that focuses on no-fault injury. I submitted the application for the articles of organization myself, following the steps available on the internet— and it worked. I was practicing and getting paid.

Despite the fatigue from working five days a week at my employed position and one day a week at my new busy practice, the excitement at seeing my business bring in revenue motivated me to continue. I bought a website domain and launched a website. I ordered signs and business cards. I hired a consulting company to complete the credentialing process so I could later accept health insurances. I had so many questions about running a business, but no one I knew had the answers. Everyone in my circle was an employee, not an entrepreneur.

Until I met Dr. Una. After listening to her podcast for months, I enrolled in the EntreMD Business School in June 2021. Enrollment gave me access to additional podcasts and lessons, as well as a tribe of colleagues who routinely shared their wins and business tips.

With advice from the EntreMD tribe, I took action steps to grow my business. I hired a part-time virtual assistant to manage social media. I learned to use software for bookkeeping. I shared the news with incredulous family members who were in awe at how quickly my practice went from nothing to something profitable.

The practice was lucrative, but my schedule was packed. So I cut my employed hours and became part time. With my new free time, I resumed some hobbies and began planning a medical mission trip for 2022. I had reached a state of equilibrium in my work life that I felt was sustainable. My prayers were answered.

However, as the revenue came in, so did the denials. Over $6,000 in unpaid revenue from a specific insurance company led to investigating and arbitrating. A lawyer confirmed their reason for denial was legitimate.

In New York State, medical offices must be registered as a PLLC, not simply an LLC. The title of "medical" or "medicine" must be in the name of the business entity. And the business must be registered with the Office of Professions.

My practice had the wrong corporate structure.

Some would even say that my practice was fraudulent.

Shock. Shame. Imposter.

How foolish to file the articles of organization by myself instead of with a CPA.

And it must now all be *redone*:

- New articles of organization
- New tax ID
- New bank account
- New website domain
- New social media accounts (Instagram, Facebook, Gmail, Pinterest, and YouTube)
- New marketing
- New group NPI, malpractice, contracts, letterhead
- And the worst part—*new credentialing*

The list goes on…

After putting over $3,000 into a ten-month-long-pandemic-delayed credentialing process, I had to cut my losses and step away. All the time and money saved by "doing it myself" was now lost in uncollected revenue and wasted credentialing.

How do I fix this? Do I change my business name completely? Do I discard a year's worth of work and start from square one? Do I switch to a PC or PLLC? Keep the LLC for something else?

The darkness pulled me into paralyzing shame and self-pity. I missed deadlines and goals. I almost missed out on the opportunity to have this chapter in this book.

Scrolling through the wins of our colleagues on social media was difficult to bear, but their uplifting messages were difficult to ignore. My colleague Dr. Catherine Toomer shared an empowering post in our Facebook group: "Do it now, do it wrong. Then do it again. Better."

In EBS class that week, our business coach Dr. Una said, "Don't cry over an unmet goal. Keep moving forward."

That was all I needed to hear.

A light shone through. The days spent in self-pity were enough. I didn't kill anyone. This wasn't malpractice. It was a simple mistake that could be corrected.

I terminated the consulting company on good terms, recognizing that the business paid for my mistakes and I still made a solid profit for the year, when many others are struggling to survive this post-pandemic resignation economy.

I consulted my CPA and made a plan to move forward. Sure, we'll have to re-create the business, but we also have an opportunity at a do-over. New name. New brand.

Mistakes will be made. Lessons will be learned. And we will share those hard-learned lessons with generations to come.

Do it wrong. Then do it again... Better.

Author: Dr. Betsy Varghese

Dr. Betsy Varghese is a family physician with fellowship training in geriatrics. She is the founder and CEO of Wellspring Health, a private practice in New York focusing on wellness. She is also the director of Education and Volunteer Services at the JPA health center, where she has served the community as a primary care physician for over ten years.

Dr. Varghese is a designated civil surgeon, a certified yoga instructor, and is pursuing a certification in massage therapy. She also loves to travel. You can find her on Instagram: @well springhealthny.

208 · SECTION II: **STARTUPS**

CHAPTER 34

TAKE **CONTROL** OF YOUR OWN LIFE

H undreds of years ago, Isaac Newton wrote in a letter, "If I have seen further, it is by standing on the shoulders of Giants." The phrase has since become a statement to illustrate scientific progress. In my training program, the sentiment of standing on the shoulders of giants, both alive and long passed, was foundational. At a subconscious level, I wondered if I would ever be enough to embody such a standard.

In the society of medicine, we are taught that to help others, we must look to the wisdom of those who came before us, those giants. We do what our senior residents, teachers, and attendings tell us to do. We follow the protocols devised by intelligent and experienced professionals. When called upon, we cite the papers we have memorized, what journal they come from, and who the authors are, all in our crumpled, coffee-stained, short white coats. Ultimately, we put the fate of our education, our careers, and to some extent, our destiny into the hands of those with seniority.

We assume that they know better and that they will mold, nurture, and guide us in the right direction.

However, to truly succeed and thrive, you must take control of your own life and sometimes even break some of the established rules to move the field forward. In the end, no matter how much your mentors help you along the way, only you can be the giant in your life.

Throughout my training and even into my first job, the paradigm of following the advice and instruction of others served me well, but at the same time, it was holding me back without me even knowing it. I did whatever my superiors told me to do to be successful. I worked as hard as I could, even to the point of sacrificing myself. My family, my friends, my interests, and even my health were put second on the list behind my job. Because that's what they did.

It was grueling, but I was always driven by the dream that one day, when I became a partner in a practice, I would be successful, just like them. I would finally be the one advising and making decisions to help patients, employees, and other physicians find their way. So I slogged on, relying on the attendings, residency leaders, mentors, and eventually shareholders in my group to decide when that moment would come for me.

After years of following other people's advice and instruction, all while sacrificing my life, I finally woke up and decided I'd had enough of working toward the life I dreamed of. It was time for me to live the life I wanted right now. I realized the people who had control over my way of practicing medicine and my life weren't me.

It wasn't in their best interest, nor was it their responsibility to make me feel worthy, fulfilled, or successful. It was my responsibility. I needed to take control. And I was just as capable as they were.

Getting myself to believe that was the hardest part in taking control of my own success because it meant that I had to take all the responsibility that comes with control. I realized that I relied on other authority figures because I didn't actually believe in myself. Believing in myself—now that took a lot of courage. This was my biggest hurdle: to believe that I was brave enough, smart enough, strong enough. That I could learn how to run a business, manage and grow money instead of more debt, and truly take care of myself.

I started to ask for what I believed was the best next step. And when my current authority figures didn't agree, I realized I might be just as smart, or maybe even smarter, than they are. In fact, I realized that compared to me, they might not be giants at all.

As my destiny would have it, I began to make bold moves. I quit the practice that I had dreamed of being a shareholder in, and I founded my own corporation. In the first year on my own, I made almost as much income as I would have made as an employee, while practicing medicine on my terms. And I gained so much fulfillment from it. I realized that I truly loved helping others in my own unique way. For the first time in my life, I was unencumbered by outdated rules that didn't serve me. This newfound sense of empowerment and fulfillment led me to found my second company, a success coaching company for other intelligent and ambitious women.

Now I work, grow, and thrive in only the way I choose, in the way that is best for me. And no one can take that away from me. I don't feel trapped by someone else's rules: that I have to stay until the boss leaves, that I have to write a note in someone else's format. Now when I stay up late, it's because my passion and my vision lift me to work hard. My life is amazing, I am thriving, and I am so thankful that I dared to create it.

Taking control was exhilarating. And terrifying. I didn't know anything about how to start or run a practice and business in my own field, much less in a completely different industry. But I gained the belief that I could learn how to do things I never thought I could before. This made me unstoppable and any dream possible. I can do anything.

I know that you can too. Don't let other people take charge of your destiny. You are brilliant and skilled in unique ways. Take charge of what you want to accomplish and how you live your life. What would it feel like to have a thriving business where you help others the way you always wanted, without having to do it someone else's way, under someone else's watch, on someone else's dime? Imagine living the life you dream of and helping your patients or your clients with standards and style that are all your own. All you need to do is take control of your own life. Don't doubt your worthiness or your ability because you are indeed a giant too.

Author: Dr. Johanna Moore

Dr. Johanna B. Moore is a triple board-certified pathologist and laboratory medical director in San Luis Obispo, California. She is also the founder of She Is Money, a success strategy and coaching membership for high-achieving women who want to ditch overwhelm and find their own versions of success. She has served as a guest on many podcasts and hosts the *Your Version of Success Podcast*.

Dr. Moore lives with her husband, twins, mother, and furry family in Pismo Beach, California. For a dash of success strategy and inspiration, you can follow her on Instagram: @sheismoney.llc.

SECTION II AUTHORS

Dr. Nikita Bhakta Shah

Dr. Ndidiamaka Obadan

Dr. Funke Afolabi-Brown

Dr. Barbara Joy Jones-Parks

Dr. Alicia Shelly

Dr. La Toya Luces-Sampson

Dr. Jeannie Collins Lawrence

Dr. Shenelle Wilson

Dr. Olabisi Badmus

Dr. Violina Bhattacharyya, FAAP

Dr. Rebecca W. Lauderdale

Dr. Erin Mayfield

Dr. Betsy Varghese

Dr. Johanna Moore

Dr. Kristi L. Kozlov, FAAO

THRIVING AS A PHYSICIAN ENTREPRENEUR

t's no secret that being a business owner comes with challenges. We have been sold a lie that doctors don't make good entrepreneurs, but the physicians in this section throw that myth right out of the window.

The truth is, doctors make the best entrepreneurs. Business skills are learnable. Doctors know all too well about sacrifice, digesting a lot of knowledge, and doing things afraid. Business is no different; in fact, it's easier than medical school.

I want to ask you, "What is possible for you as a physician entrepreneur?" In the following stories, doctors share how they leveraged mindset, community, and practical strategies to thrive as entrepreneurs. May they inspire you to dream of a better future, armed with the knowledge that it's actually doable. They are all the proof you need.

CHAPTER 35

KNOW YOUR
SUPERPOWER

W as I scared? Of course. But when you have the confidence that what you are doing is right, it can feel like there is no choice.

Although charging an annual fee to be part of our pediatric practice seemed "out of the box" and foreign to our market, if we were going to run the practice the way we felt was consistent with the model we wanted (more time for visits and patients having reasonable access to their physicians), we knew that the traditional insurance model just wouldn't work. With concierge not what we were looking for, it was either this way or no way.

I think a lot of physicians feel that way, like things are unsustainable the way they are. Crazy hours, constant calls, weekend duties, seemingly endless messages from patients, staff issues—it wasn't going to work unless we did this. But of course we were hesitant and second-guessed ourselves.

Sending the email the first year was like asking someone out on a date—so much riding on it! But we persisted, and it went great! Fifteen years later, I wouldn't have done it any other way. Having launched this successful practice model, I am bringing that same bravado to opening a wellness center for adults. Once you take the first leap, it definitely gets easier!

The secret of my success as an entrepreneur is twofold. The first is confidence. You are a physician, so know your worth. Recent graduates come out with debt in excess of $200K–$500K, and a lot of hard work went into that degree. I always felt like I gave up my twenties. When all my friends were living exciting lives—going to each other's weddings, traveling, having lots of random exciting sex—I was either in the library, on call, exhausted post call, or spending my precious free time with my neglected, often resentful family and close friends.

Trust me, that was not a plea for pity. As physicians, we pay up front and reap the rewards later with job security, more than ample income, and often a better quality of life than other professions. As my mentor Dr. Una points out, very very few people statistically are admitted to and matriculate from medical school, so *own it*! That confidence in your abilities is what will help you take the leap you need to as an entrepreneur.

I *love* telling people I am a doctor. For most, it means that I am a nice, brilliant, charitable person—and they treat me better than if they thought I was a lawyer! Truth, right? And if you are bold, they will be more inclined to help you or have faith in your entrepreneurial journey. You may be looking for funders, and you would be surprised how many conversations the MD can start.

The second part of my success equation is valuing myself. Lacking a strong sense of self-worth permeates every part of your life, so amortize your worth. I personally think we are all worth $500/hr, but if you make the average salary of a physician (around $300,000), then you make $150/hr—so anyone whom you pay less than that is saving you time and money.

Don't let gender roles determine what jobs you do. If you don't *love* it, then pay someone else to do it! Get a scribe (let's be honest, who *loves* doing notes?), cook, and nanny you love. I regret having made some decisions to save money when I could have made some choices that made my life easier.

At work, set boundaries and get really good at trying to make it fun and expressing what you need to make your day easier. Other people, especially administration, don't read our minds or even begin to understand the stresses physicians are under, so be the squeaky wheel. If you get negative feedback, it's likely a sign that you should move on…

It is your right to be an intrapreneur or an entrepreneur, and don't let anyone tell you otherwise! Don't downplay your ideas because they won't be profitable right away. Not every idea will turn into a raving success, but some of them will, so go for it. They say the lightbulb was just one of hundreds of inventions that Thomas Edison created. What if he stopped before that one, discouraged? If you have a great idea for a book, then set aside time for it, even though you are paying a sitter $25/hr or cook, and so forth. Time is money! You owe it to yourself to try to build on your big ideas.

Be open to allowing the world to give you the respect you have earned with your hard work! You are amazing, smart, generous, and caring—own your worth and demand respect. We get so caught up in our frenzied lives, especially if we are assuming the childcare, CEO, and house manager roles. There is barely space to breathe! But carve it out, let go of the traditional roles, and work in your zone of genius.

Surround yourself with people who believe in you as well— partners, parents, friends, and so forth. It will help to have their love and support to accomplish your dreams. If you have someone close to you who just can't see your gifts or has a very difficult time getting out of their comfort zone, then don't make them someone you confide in.

I have always had naysayers in my life. Although it can be aggravating—the haters got to hate—I tune them out and turn to those who are my cheerleaders and who also can give me counsel when I need it. If I had given up on my dream of the wellness center when people at work looked at me like I had two heads, it would never be coming to fruition the way it has.

For my second life relationship chapter, I am with someone who celebrates my dreams and helps me see them to completion. She doesn't view them as "crazy" but calls me "brilliant." Hugely supportive, and I feel so lucky.

Manifesting your creative dreams is in your grasp, I promise. And yet, she persisted. Do it. Baby steps, meaningful conversations with our partners and supporters. Put it out in the universe when there is a calm moment. Your circle loves you and wants to support you, and if they don't, send them out into orbit (obviously tricky with family, but some space can be helpful).

You have worked so far to get here—make it your dream life! If you are passionate and informed about it, you will succeed. You have already proven you have the tools for success with your medical degree. And if you are a true entrepreneur, the thoughts won't go away until you realize them!

Author: Dr. Nikki Gorman

Dr. Nikki Gorman, MD, is an entrepreneur at heart! As a pediatrician, she loves kids but never lost her desire to help make the world a better place by creating businesses. She is the founder of Westport Medical and Wellness Center and hosts wellness retreats for physicians. Dr. Nikki lives in Westport, Connecticut with her amazing daughter (her two super sons have flown the nest) and two adorable dogs.

She loves to entertain, so please watch her! And hopefully, you will learn a little in the process. Find her on TikTok: @drnikki_.

CHAPTER 36

BELIEF AND
SELF-IDENTITY

I didn't come from a family of physicians. My father is a business professor, who encouraged all of his children to get engineering degrees in college and pursue business. During my childhood, my mother was an entrepreneur, who wished we would go to medical school since she saw being a physician as a secure and well-paying profession.

After college, I applied to multiple jobs, but having graduated in 2001, just after the tech bust, I ended up deciding to go to medical school. When I finished fellowship training, I knew I wanted to not only practice medicine but that I also wanted to learn the business side of running a private practice. I had even considered starting my own practice but decided I wasn't quite bold enough to take that on straight out of training.

I ended up choosing a job with a private practice owned by an ophthalmologist, who said he was looking for someone to share the responsibilities of the business and that I could become a partner whenever I was ready. I got records of prior tax filings and other documents to review the financials of the business before accepting the job. It was a well-run practice with a team atmosphere that even included staff bonuses if revenue targets were met.

Unfortunately, at some point I realized that I didn't see a future for myself at that practice. I decided to leave and return to my hometown, where I took a job with a hospital system to give myself time to get established in the community prior to striking it out on my own.

Working at the hospital solidified my desire to work for myself. I had very little autonomy or control and no voice. I was held accountable for results with no control over the process. I started creating plans to leave the hospital by the end of 2020 and start my private practice in 2021.

And then the COVID-19 pandemic changed everything.

I realized medicine wasn't as secure a profession as I thought. I was thankful I hadn't already started my private practice, where I might have leases to pay and staff to support with no income due to the shutdown. But I was also worried that I might find myself drafted to working outside my scope of practice, without proper protective equipment, and having to risk my own health and maybe even life. When I took the Physician Well-Being Index Assessment in 2020, I scored "extremely low" such that when my score displayed, information for the help and crisis lines appeared.

I knew something needed to change, and I started looking for options. One turning point came when I discovered coaching and The Life Coach School. When certification to become a life coach was offered in September, I decided to do it for my own growth. What I discovered was that I love coaching. The entrepreneur in me could see all the benefits of starting a life coaching business with lower overhead and less regulation, compared to starting a medical private practice with much higher overhead and lots of regulation. I listed the pros and cons, and starting a life coaching business had so many benefits, except one thing—it sounded a little crazy.

After spending eight years in a medical school and graduate school, four years in residency, and two years in fellowship, I identify as a physician. I'm proud to be a physician. And as a physician, I believe in the practice of medicine. When I prescribe a drug, I believe that its effects will address the condition I am treating. When I perform surgery, I am directly doing an intervention that fixes the problem. When a patient questions my medical recommendations in clinic, I don't make it mean anything about me.

At the end of my six-month coaching certification program, I was only starting to identify as a life coach. I knew the value of coaching from my own experience of receiving coaching. There are peer-reviewed journal articles that showed as little as six coaching sessions was enough to significantly reduce burnout. There were some very successful physician coaches charging thousands of dollars for their programs. But I had a hard time believing that people would want to pay me to be their own coach. Why would someone choose me instead of the established coaching programs already out there? And if they did choose me, could I truly give them the transformation they were looking for?

To market myself and sell coaching, I had to believe in the value of my coaching, in my ability to coach other people to reach their goals and shift their mindset. I had to believe that there are people who would connect with me and want to pay me to coach them. I had to put myself out there so these people could find me.

I had a ton of insecurity. I was never popular or charismatic. I wasn't well-known in any circles, in medicine or outside of medicine. I didn't have a lot of connections. I wasn't good with social media. I barely posted on Facebook and didn't use Instagram, Twitter, TikTok, or whatever else there is out there.

What I am is disciplined and determined. And so, I got started. I started a YouTube channel and started putting out a video every week. I joined physician groups on Facebook and started contributing regularly. I started my own Facebook group where I post daily. I attended online conferences and went to every virtual networking event I could to get out and meet people. I asked to be a guest on podcasts so I could spread my message. I invested in my business to get the information, skills, and support to be successful.

Eventually, people started reaching out to ask about what I offer and were interested in working with me. And then, I got that first client who said yes! Soon, I had multiple clients. With each paying client, my belief in myself as a life coach and entrepreneur grew, and I began to truly believe that my success is inevitable.

Author: Dr. Elizabeth Chiang, PhD

Dr. Elizabeth Chiang, also known as Elisa, is an ophthalmologist, fellowship-trained oculoplastic surgeon, and life coach who reached millionaire status three years after finishing her medical training. She is the founder and CEO of Grow Your Wealthy Mindset, where she helps other physicians overcome burnout, achieve their goals, and build their wealth. Dr. Chiang has also been a guest on numerous podcasts and is the host of her own YouTube channel.

She lives in her hometown of Cleveland, Ohio, with her husband. You can follow her on Facebook: @ElisaChiang.

CHAPTER 37

CREATING THE LIFE THAT YOU **WANT** TO LIVE

"What were you thinking? You're *fine*. Come back for a *real* emergency." I found myself yelling at my patient, at least in my head. I was five months pregnant, going on seventy-two hours working in the ER, stuck in the aftermath of a Category 3 hurricane, unable to get home even if I wanted to.

This isn't me. What happened to my empathy?

I was living halfway around the world from my aging parents in what I had thought was a dream job. I had worked so hard to get here, spending over a dozen years and a quarter million dollars in student loans just to get to the "finish line." But although I loved saving lives in the ER, I felt that I had to find a balance between family obligations and a better quality of life.

Family came first, so I left practicing medicine as I knew it to move halfway around the world with my husband and two young kids in tow. This was literally living outside of my comfort zone, and I had to learn new skills, starting with the language, as I hadn't lived in Japan since I was a child. I knew nothing about running my father's cancer immunotherapy clinic and even less about regenerative medicine, but I slowly learned about growing immune cells in our lab, doing clinical research, managing employees, and running a business.

The stress of this new life started taking a toll on my health, but I buried my discomfort, thinking that this was best for my family. By the time I looked up, I realized I was again getting burned out; I had high cholesterol and blood pressure and was fifty pounds overweight. The fear and doubt that I had made the wrong decision set in—that feeling of being stuck. Maybe I was too old to change my job, change my life. I felt that sinking feeling in the pit of my stomach that maybe I wouldn't be able to provide for my family in the way I'd always wanted to.

But then, like fog lifting before my eyes, I had a "midlife awakening." *What am I doing? How do I craft my life in the way I want to live? How do I find balance?*

First, I needed to address my own physical and mental health. I discovered coaching and lifestyle medicine, lost the weight, and regained my health.

In the process, I realized there was a disconnect in the way we were treating patients and preventing illness. Thinking back on my ER days, I realized that 80 percent of what I had been treating was potentially preventable—even 30–50 percent of all cancers are preventable. I began giving public lectures on lifestyle medicine and began coaching clients on how to live their best healthy lives.

Our private practice specializes in cancer vaccines and immunotherapy. This amazing treatment is patented in a dozen countries and is not available anywhere else in the world. This groundbreaking approach to treating cancer uses the patient's own immune cells to recognize and destroy cancer. I realized that my lifestyle medicine coaching was uniquely aligned with helping our cancer patients with nutrition, exercise, sleep, and stress reduction. I began helping patients thrive—not just survive beyond their diagnosis.

Being able to see these achievements as successes strangely did not happen until I allowed myself to be open to sharing, to come out of my introverted shell, and to join a community of amazing like-minded physicians. They showed me the way to own my voice and truly become an entrepreneur.

I recognize now that in these past years, I had become a research doctor, publishing article after article on early cancer diagnosis using liquid biopsy and genetic testing. I published amazing case studies of patients who had no evidence of disease after using our immunotherapy treatments. I researched using cutting-edge technology on a patient's own circulating tumor cells to create a new type of cancer vaccine. I, an ER doc, with no official training in the field of oncology, was given the opportunity to coauthor chapters in oncology textbooks.

I went from being an employed worker bee to running a regenerative medicine laboratory and a private practice. Thanks to the support of this group, I embraced public speaking, and I have now spoken internationally in multiple languages. I learned that speaking with an accent is not something to be ashamed of but a sign of bravery.

I have been interviewed for magazine articles and featured on podcasts. I am recording videos to teach patients what they can do through lifestyle medicine to become healthier and reduce cancer risk. I've started my own blog on my personal website and have published articles about lifestyle medicine.

In my coaching, I have transformed lives, helping people to reverse their metabolic syndrome, lose weight, normalize cholesterol, decrease inflammation, and reduce their cancer risk. My clients have reported not just feeling better physically but are emotionally less sad and anxious, more confident, having better relationships with themselves and others, and just thriving beyond their expectations.

I have unknowingly become an expert. I realize that my voice matters and that by not speaking out, I was doing a disservice to others who could be helped by what I had to say. Most importantly, I am healing myself and finding my humanity again.

No matter what the future holds, I know now that I can continue to evolve and reinvent myself at any point in my career. I am energized, uplifted, and humbled by being able to make a difference in people's lives.

We are physicians. We can do hard things. We can heal ourselves and our patients and, in doing so, regain our empathy and compassion. We can follow our passions, love what we do, and create the life that we want to live.

Author: Dr. Minako Abe

Dr. Minako Abe has dual board certifications in emergency medicine and lifestyle medicine. She is the CEO of Lifestyle Medicine Japan and vice-president of the Tokyo Cancer Clinic. In addition to providing cutting-edge immune cell therapies for cancer, she coaches patients and survivors in lifestyle and mindset so that they thrive, not just survive. She is a published researcher and an international speaker.

Dr. Abe lives in Tokyo, Japan with her husband, two wonderful children, and a chubby chihuahua. You can follow her on Instagram: @dr.minako.

CHAPTER 38

THE SECOND TIME AROUND IS **BETTER** THAN THE FIRST TIME

I am Rose Marie Thomas, pediatrician of twenty-five years, CEO and founder of Frontier Kids Care, on the beautiful twin island of Trinidad and Tobago. I unlock full potential by dispensing "distilled wisdom" to help parents who are anxious about their child's well-being in health, learning, and parenting so that the future child is a gift to the world!

However, in the early hours of the morning while on call as a resident, I only dreamed about having my own practice. It would be holistic and serve many families. I was also an intuitive artist, and I wanted to bring the love of literature, music, art, and design to the creative process of building a practice.

When I started Frontier Kids Care, I blended the unique West Indian art of storytelling with humor, play, and standard pediatric practice and evolved to become a dispenser of "distilled wisdom." I brought the lessons learned from difficult passages of my life to the table and was able to help anxious parents become good enough parents.

There were key pieces of the puzzle missing, however, that I could not articulate. I served well, but despite all my experience, I struggled to scale my business.

And I was not prepared for the upcoming retirement phase of life. I lacked some financial skills, but more importantly, I had no idea that the dreams and services that I had curated over the years had so much worth.

The crisis of the COVID-19 pandemic gave me my new mantra: Never waste a good crisis.

And what a crisis it was! Because of severe and ongoing lockdowns, parents faced economic and physical distancing challenges. Children were missing school, depression and anxiety were soaring, yet families were missing in action.

At Frontier Kids Care, we too faced a crisis, as our fault lines became deep fissures: our revenue plummeted for months on end, and I faced the difficult task of steering this "enterprise" to new frontiers.

I was preoccupied with how to bring in money, control expenses, and schedule kids to come in. I knew I had to do something, but what and how?

I had all these fears that kept me going in circles:

- Was I good enough? (small island syndrome)
- Could I overcome the terror of coming out of my comfort zone to "market" myself and my practice?
- Could I delegate to others so that I could stay in my "zone of genius"? What was that anyway?
- Was I a doctor or an artist, or could I be both?
- Would I be able to retire comfortably soon?
- Would patients disappear if I charged more for the services I provided?
- How could I set goals to improve my business and follow-through?

The dancer in me pivoted with extraordinary effort, finding new ways to generate passive income, control expenses, address scheduling problems to bring in existing patients, and get before the eyes of new ones. I kept my solid business foundation but worked on the harder task of renovation by embracing new technologies like online payments, telehealth, and social media to meet patients where they were.

I stumbled upon *The EntreMD Podcast* and knew immediately that this spoke to my own entrepreneurial struggle. I listened to every single episode and took notes. I was so excited because finally, someone got me, and I joined the EntreMD Business School (EBS) right away.

What happened here?

I truly had a mindset transplant that left me with two major gifts.

First, there was nothing wrong with being a multi-talented physician who loved dancing, literature, and designing spaces and businesses. What I perceived as an obstacle was actually a huge gift, and EBS guided me to unwrap it, own it, and recognize the value that this brings to my practice and life. I discovered my zone of genius!

Second, I got to understand the immense value of my dreams and was given the tools to convert them into goals, build a relationship with them, and execute them to serve and earn well.

At EBS, I received mentorship, guidance, a blueprint, and a team of fearless comrades that I could trust, share with, emulate, and even mentor. I embraced a new mantra: *I could do hard things*.

Let me humble brag a bit about the new practice and the new me:

- The doors of my practice remained open, while others closed.
- I served during the pandemic with a new telehealth platform and have a new vertical source of income.
- I delegated marketing so that I could work instead on revenue-generating activities.
- I overcame the fear of networking, started asking people and patients to work with me, and got over twenty five-star reviews!
- I distilled my message to my ideal client, and now I regularly speak to them on our new YouTube channel, Frontier TV. We have over twenty-five episodes.

- We upscaled social media by doubling Facebook engagement, and we're in front of new eyes on Instagram and LinkedIn. Just imagine, Frontier Kids Care is everywhere!
- We continued to serve the nation through difficult times, while we patiently awaited a bright financial future, because we'd done the hard work.

On a personal note, I embraced my authentic self: the belief that this Afro-West Indian female doctor/artist in her early sixties could stand up and be counted, because I still had a lot to offer the world. I embraced the fear and excitement of the journey to this new frontier and followed my own advice of taking life easy when the difficulties presented themselves.

The second time around, Frontier Kids Care has been reinvented and reimagined to suit the present times and needs. This captain can finally see the new horizon and is becoming the doctor I dreamed of, with a business legacy.

The second time around is going to be amazing and definitely better than the first time!

Author: Dr. Rose Marie Thomas

Dr. Rose Marie Thomas is a veteran pediatrician in her solo pediatric practice, Frontier Kids Care. She is super proud of being able to keep the practice open during the pandemic lockdown and to grow her social media presence exponentially.

Dr. Thomas is proud of her legacy as a premier pediatric practice in Trinidad and Tobago, where she is also a parent to two emerging young adults. You can find her "distilled wisdom" on YouTube at Frontier Kids Care.

CHAPTER 39

UNCERTAINTY HOLDS **INFINITE** POTENTIAL

'␣ve been enamored with holistic healing and spirituality since I was a kid growing up in India. I read dozens of mind-body well-being books in college. I learned how to meditate and used those skills to get into medical school. During medical school and residency, I quashed those skills and ideas down so I could fit in, but they didn't die.

Years later, I found myself feeling stuck in a well-paying, hospital-owned outpatient clinic. In fact, I felt stuck in almost every area of my life. I had no idea how to balance my roles as wife, mom, physician, friend, and daughter. I felt overwhelmed much of the time.

I gravitated back to my daily meditation practice. This small self-care commitment created big ripples. I took deep dives into studying meditation and the sister science of ayurveda. I changed how I practiced medicine. I was juggling my roles imperfectly but felt grounded. I thought I might stay at this job forever.

But medicine began changing rapidly in 2016. My unique way of practicing and my autonomy were dissolving in a metric-driven world. At first, I was in denial. *Surely, someone will fix the mess*, I thought. *I'm supposed to practice here forever.* But the constriction felt worse and worse. I had outgrown the box.

I wanted to serve people in a way that felt more authentic to me, but I was afraid and worried about the uncertainty of starting my own business. I dealt with fear by distracting myself, taking exotic vacations, and planning elaborately busy weekends. I contemplated and dismissed business ideas hundreds of times. But my dreams of helping people heal holistically came back every single Monday. I dreamed about teaching meditation as I drove to work. The idea seemed ludicrous—straying from the mainstream and being an entrepreneur with an uncertain future.

I was at a CME meeting, feeling like a hostage, when I ran into my friend, who was a successful physician entrepreneur. He said, "C'mon in, the water's just fine." After years of desperate deliberation, I knew then that I was taking the plunge. I was excited and nervous.

My entrepreneurial path has been nonlinear. At first, I started a Direct Care practice with coaching, which was hugely underpriced. This was an amazing deal for patients but a lousy one for me. I floundered financially.

My trajectory changed when I decided to invest in my personal and professional growth by joining EntreMD Business School (EBS) and becoming a certified coach. I got coached, watched other physician entrepreneurs, and finally discovered my value and my worth. With my mindset shifts, I made offers to new clients for 10x what I had charged patients just the month before. I was shaking with fear, but I did it anyway. And many clients said yes!

I didn't stop there. I moved past my terror of appearing on screens. I did videos on Facebook and on my YouTube channel. My ego was bruised many times, but I kept coming back to my inner knowing… *My people are looking for me.* And it was true—more clients found me.

I asked to be on bigger stages, like national summits and retreats. I was offered coveted speaking spots. I've been a guest on fourteen podcasts and counting. I work hard to deliver high value on every stage.

More doors have opened. I was featured by Chopra Global on "teacher spotlight" in 2021—handpicked out of 4,500 teachers globally. Separately, I had the honor of meeting Deepak Chopra and Mallika Chopra in person at a small gathering, and the Chopra organization gave me my biggest stage yet: I was asked to teach their global community of teachers. Doing well on that large stage helped me become a more courageous and confident speaker. And it positioned me as an expert in mind-body healing and coaching.

I've learned to pivot, collaborate, and evolve faster than I imagined possible. I saw radical transformation in my private clients and knew I could coach and teach a group of women ready for transformation. Collaborating with my friend Courtenay, we created a program called Ready to Thrive.

I learned so much from the challenges of that launch. I ran multiple webinars, sent out dozens of emails and social media posts with the goal of serving ten women, but twenty-four hours before our program began, we had only five registered. I wanted to give up, but we pushed until the final hour. Finally, we enrolled eleven women!

Having learned from this program, I'm building a more robust coaching and meditation membership, which will launch soon. I hope to scale this quickly.

I've created multiple verticals in my business, Optimal Wellness. I facilitate group meditations every week, and I offer one-on-one coaching, plus meditation teaching. I partnered with my physician friend Tea to offer an in-person retreat locally, and we created an irresistible offer that worked well for serving and earning. We sold all twenty spots of our first in-person retreat in twenty-four hours! There's already a long wait list for the next retreat.

As I evolve, I've stopped making money mean more than what it is. I moved my one-on-one pricing to one that feels like a win-win for all. When a client has invested a few thousand dollars, she will show up differently and get different results than if she spent a fraction of that money. It's a liberating discovery.

I make mistakes, and I have successes. I'm always learning and evolving from a place of self-compassion and abundance. My practice of meditation helps keep me grounded.

Embracing uncertainty didn't come naturally, but staying open has helped me to tap into my infinite potential—my seemingly far-fetched dream is now a reality. I help people heal in a way that feels more authentic to me. I am becoming more vibrant every day. My journey is messy, and I know my future is uncertain, but I wouldn't change a thing.

Your infinite potential is waiting to be unlocked too. Are you contemplating jumping out? C'mon in, the water's just fine.

Author: Dr. Rashmi Schramm

Dr. Rashmi Schramm is a board-certified family physician, a certified integrative health coach, and a Chopra Certified Meditation and Ayurveda teacher. She is the founder of Optimal Wellness, where she helps busy women tap into inner peace and power so they can live more energetic and purposeful lives. Finally, Rashmi is an avid speaker who also leads group coaching/meditation programs, in-person retreats, and private coaching.

Rashmi lives with her husband, their two daughters, and their dog in Saint Johns, Florida, where they spend most of their free time outdoors. You can find her on Facebook as Rashmi Schramm.

CHAPTER 40

BEING **YOURSELF** IS THE BEST MEDICINE

I tried to leave medicine before I was even fully in it. Although I had discovered that medicine, and more importantly health, was always in me, as I approached high school graduation, I was tired from a large volume of AP classes and daunted by a decade-long trajectory of school. I decided to find a four-year degree that would offer me access to health in a more efficient fashion.

During opening-day college introductions, I knew I was in the wrong place. My dreams evolved from the practice of veterinary to human medicine. I greeted the teacher and students, then excused myself to the counselor's office to change my major to pre-med.

An accelerated course and early admission found me at the doorstep of medical school at twenty-one years old, not yet ready to cross that threshold. I deferred for a year, planning to compete in a triathlon. One week in, I tore my ACL. This injury was a guardrail that kept me on the path to medicine.

Osteopathic medical school resonated with my understanding of how health could be honored, fostered, nurtured, discovered, engaged, and encouraged. Residency did not. Six months in, I approached the director of medical education, thanking him for the opportunity and announcing my departure for a life of racing, training, and engaging health through fitness.

Drawing on many years counseling students and residents through major life decisions, he encouraged me to pause and reconsider. I offered the solution of launching a new residency program on a nearly impossible timeline. Surprisingly, we pulled it off, and I was on track in neuromusculoskeletal and osteopathic manipulative medicine.

Training in this specialty resurrected a degree of resonance, enough to help me hear the melody and play along for a while. I was good at my work, and my patients did well. I ascended the leadership ranks within my clinic and in education. But I was not satisfied; I knew there was more. While I spent my time focusing on the health of my patients, I could see that the health of the system was waning.

There was dis-ease and dysfunction. Physicians were frustrated. Staff were overworked and underpaid. Residents felt unseen and unheard. Students were chasing goals with a haste fueled by growing debt. I hit barricades of institutional inertia, cultural conditioning, and self-judgment.

I changed course to private practice with slivers of solace. The resonance echoed but quietly. I joined a small group where I had autonomy and support. The resonance rang with greater clarity.

I noticed that my partners seemed to gain from each encounter, to be energized and fulfilled by one-to-one patient care. I wondered what was wrong with me that I could not share the same joy from an engagement I truly valued—I had lost touch with the resonance.

Then another injury sidelined me from exercise, forcefully eliminating my primary method of escape from the unsettled, dissatisfied feelings that chased me from one idea to the next, without anything taking shape. The resonance was trying to come through, but I was not listening.

It took a global pandemic and a temporary closure of my clinic for me to finally hear with clarity the message that had been playing for so long: "I am not going back." I was no longer willing to be anchored to a system that did not reflect the health that I saw, felt, and knew in the world around me.

One week later, I was in my first coaching certification class. The invitation was made to focus on what was going well for the person, that they were whole, worthy, and perfect just as they were, and that discovery of any answers was going to come from the person themselves, not from me. I was ready at that moment to embrace the course I had always been on: To honor each individual. To see their health. To reflect their unlimited potential. To welcome them with their inherent self-healing capacity. To realize how amazing they already were.

This was medicine. I did not have to leave; I just had to be fully myself and welcome others to do the same. Trying to be like anyone else led to constant dissatisfaction. Not listening to my instincts and strengths led to persistent dissonance. Attempting to fit into a system that did not uphold my mission, vision, and values led to recurrent damage to mind, body, and spirit.

Trusting myself—my sense, my dream, my drive—was the beginning. Finding a supportive community, experienced mentors, and action plans created clarity and led me to see that the path to honor health was one of entrepreneurship. Upholding the tenets that drew me into osteopathic medicine two decades earlier served as the foundation for creating programs that truly supported health, and satisfaction emerged.

Tuning into my strengths in inspiration, revolution, and collaboration brought resonance, showing me I was a leader in bringing health to medicine. Acknowledging that I do not have to adapt to a system that does not mirror my mission and values opened room for healing—body, mind, and spirit. Now my work is in the practice of medicine as I always knew it to be: of, about, for, and focused on health.

Training others.

Seeing possibility.

Honoring inherent wisdom.

Coaching is medicine. Medicine is health. Health is here.

Since closing my clinic doors over one year ago, I have facilitated programs for more than 500 physicians at all stages of education, training, and practice. I have written and spoken on dozens of platforms. I have created contentment in my life with alignment of vision, maintenance of mission, freedom of schedule, outlets for creativity, and continued dedication to health.

Trust your instincts. Honor your strengths. Learn to identify when discomfort is from the heavy lifting of good, hard work and when it is from the dissonance of a system that does not honor your value and values.

Be yourself, and in belonging, *be health.*

Author: Dr. Amelia L. Bueche

Dr. Amelia Bueche specializes in neuromusculoskeletal and osteopathic manipulative medicine and is the creative director of This Osteopathic Life: For the Health of All Things. She is the founder and program director of Coaching for Institutions: Bringing Health to Medicine, creating programs for physicians at all stages of education, training, and practice.

Finally, Dr. Bueche has a podcast called *This Osteopathic Life* and is a teacher, leader, and speaker, featured on stages locally and nationally.

Dr. Bueche is an athlete and active community member in Traverse City, Michigan, where she lives with her children. You can follow her on Facebook: @This Osteopathic Life.

CHAPTER 41

IMPOSTER SYNDROME AND OTHER **LIES** WE TELL OURSELVES

M y business grew from a time in my life when I was at my lowest. I was depressed, morbidly obese, an insulin-dependent diabetic, diagnosed with postpartum cardiomyopathy, and given a 50 percent chance of living five years. I was thirty-six years old with a toddler and a newborn. I was literally sick and tired. As a board-certified family medicine physician whose job it was to guide patients to their optimal health, I had failed miserably for myself. At the time, the term "imposter syndrome" wasn't widely used; otherwise, I probably would have claimed it.

When I finally had the strength to take control of my obesity, I was turned away from programs for being too high risk, so I did it on my own. I dived deep into my biopsychosocial background, lost sixty pounds in six months, got off insulin, and survived my congestive heart failure. Then I created what is now my signature wellness and weight loss program from the notes I kept during my transformation.

Over the next fifteen years, I worked exclusively as an employed physician in underserved areas. But when I tried to apply my prevention program with my patients, I became increasingly frustrated by not having time or support. My frustration in an ill-care system began taking its toll on my health, and I knew I couldn't sustain that level of stress for much longer.

I decided then that I needed my own office, but how? I googled "How to open a micropractice." The first step was "form an LLC," and so Health Wellness and Weight Loss Centers, LLC was born. I was fifty-one years old, had never worked in a private practice, let alone owned one, and was now a founder and CEO. Me?

It took me a long time to call myself an entrepreneur, a businesswoman—a boss. I wondered if I had imposter syndrome but decided there was no need to label my fear and uncertainty. I had maneuvered while scared in school, residency, and when new to medical practice, and so I did the same again with business ownership. In any other circumstance when we persevere in the face of fear and self-doubt, we call ourselves brave, not an imposter.

I have since grown to believe that giving our fear, self-doubt, and insecurities a name gives them power. Imposter syndrome is the lie we tell ourselves as an excuse for allowing fear to dictate our actions—or in my case, nonaction. The fear when starting a business, and the situations that come with it, is no different than the fear we felt when starting medical school, or when presenting a complicated patient to an attending, or the panic when running our first code. Fear, self-doubt, and insecurities did not stop us from becoming physicians, and we do not call ourselves imposter doctors, so why apply it to entrepreneurship?

By regarding fear, self-doubt, and feeling fraudulent as a syndrome, we pathologize what is a normal part of growth and achievement. Fear of new situations, fear of failing, self-doubt when facing difficulty, anxiety in places requiring our psychological protection …we all have experienced these in our professional journey.

Keep in mind, whether an "imposter" or not, when we set high goals, the questions we ask ourselves shape our path. It is in answering "How will I?" "What will I?" and "Why am I?" that we confirm our beliefs and soar, or doubt ourselves to the point of sabotage. This is human nature, not a label.

I adopted a strategy I learned in my family medicine training and had used successfully with my patients: journaling. Keeping a win, gratitude, and affirmation journal and reading the entries out loud daily helps me to hear my voice outside my head and to quiet the questioning voice inside. It reminds me of my highs when I'm feeling low, and just like how use builds muscle, over time my inner cheerleader has become the strongest voice I hear. I still have limiting thoughts, but instead of shouting like before, they whisper.

Dr. Ethan Kross is a University of Michigan psychologist and neuroscientist who specializes in emotional regulation. In his book *Chatter: The Voice in Our Head, Why It Matters, How to Harness It*, Kross states that the silent conversations we have with ourselves influence how we live our lives, and when our brain is not occupied with other tasks, talking to ourselves is our default mode. And when we talk to ourselves, we listen. Kross emphasizes that negative introspection puts our performance, decision making, relationships, happiness, and our health in jeopardy. In my opinion, claiming imposter syndrome is negative introspection with negative consequences.

If you don't tell yourself you have imposter syndrome when scared about starting a business, then you don't have it—it's that simple. But simple isn't always easy, except with practice. So practice telling yourself that your degrees are symbols of your expertise. Practice telling yourself that your story has value. Practice focusing on your wins and remembering what you say to and about yourself matters. But most importantly, remind yourself that you are a physician and have succeeded in the face of many difficult and scary situations before.

We in medicine have watched the landscape change; healthcare is now run by businesspeople, and doctors are regarded as cogs in the wheels and not the drivers of the train. Our business ownership is not only taking charge of the train but also the tracks. It's scary and at times lonely, but the autonomy is worth it. When venturing outside what we've been told is our box, we feel out of our element, but instead of calling ourselves what we are not—an imposter with a syndrome—we should celebrate what we really are: brave doctors taking medicine back.

When I finally embraced my entrepreneurial identity, I sought out a business coach specifically for doctors. I trusted the process, and within a few months, my revenue increased over 600 percent. I uncomfortably made myself more publicly visible, which led to my TEDx Talk about—wait for it—imposter syndrome.

But what really showed me the power of ownership was when my father passed away in March 2020. Three days later, I shut my office due to COVID-19, and then I shut down too. I went 100 percent virtual within a week while still reeling, yet my business grew even more. No matter what value I place on my business, I had complete autonomy when I needed it most, and that was—and is—priceless.

Author: Dr. Catherine H. Toomer

Dr. Catherine Toomer is a family medicine physician who founded Health Wellness and Weight Loss Centers to break rules and remove the shaming and overwhelm common in wellness and weight loss spaces. She developed her highly successful TOTAL Wellness + Weight Loss™ programs while losing one hundred pounds to control her diabetes, get off insulin, and survive postpartum cardiomyopathy. When not coaching, Dr. Toomer is a TEDx speaker and a popular guest on numerous podcasts, including *Black Doctors Podcast.*

Dr. Toomer is a polymath who lives in South Carolina with her husband, two labradoodles, and an empty nest. You can follow her on Facebook: @c.harmon.toomer-md.

CHAPTER 42

YOU **CHOOSE**

Follower or Impact Maker

G raduating from residency and moving to Colorado marked a
new beginning for me and my family. Great excitement and
anticipation do not fully describe the feelings I had after many
years of schooling, including residency and fellowships. I thought
I had finally arrived and could have my dream life.

But after settling into my job, passing my boards, making
friends, and managing "work-life" balance (is there such a thing?),
I still wasn't happy. I was stressed, frustrated, and frightened. I
worked hard and long hours. I was hustling between offices, always
feeling rushed and discontented. I also wanted to expand my services, which was not an option since I was one of many providers
in a large dermatology group.

After one year of unhappiness, I decided to leave for a smaller
group. I was enthusiastic about the challenge to help a fellow

dermatologist grow his practice. I hoped I would have more opportunities to grow and provide the care I imagined for my patients.

Passionately, I went above and beyond providing outstanding care, and I was delighted that patients wanted to see me. I saw thirty to forty patients daily, four and a half days a week with one assistant, and took most of the weekend calls. I even marketed the practice by giving talks and connecting with other physicians.

The practice grew big enough to require another physician and even a second location, but my job remained the same. No personal growth was available. Even though I enjoyed taking care of patients, I yearned for learning and impact. Despite the daily joy of all the success and growth of the practice, my heart was not satisfied. I was burned out.

Notwithstanding all my efforts in the practice's growth and marketing, my contributions were not recognized. I was mostly asked to follow the rules, and I had no input in development and improvement. My value system did not align with leadership, and I felt I wasn't able to utilize all my capabilities. I did not sense I was making the impact I was hoping for—I was fulfilling someone else's dream. I constantly felt I was not doing enough or not knowing enough and couldn't measure up.

After four years, I was offered a 10 percent partnership, which was a true sign that I needed to follow my own calling and start the entrepreneurial journey that I have been thinking about. I wasn't built to be contained; I was here to create, heal, and make a change.

With my husband's encouragement and help, I decided to open my own practice. Although I had many ideas on how I would run or structure a practice, I actually never had any business training, nor did I have entrepreneurs in my family. The feeling of inadequacy and the imposter syndrome were painful, and I thought I couldn't be as good as other dermatologists in town. I even thought about moving to a different state to avoid these feelings.

However, the idea of creating my own company, a place where I could finally practice the way I always wanted to, improve patients' skin health, and affect their lives, was very inspiring. After some deliberation about the name of the company, after learning online how to, we created and registered our LLC. I was scared—this is not something I had ever thought I would do with my strict medical training—but I was *very* dedicated! I was the breadwinner of our family of four, with kids ages three and seven and a graduate student husband, so failing was not an option.

Frightened and hopeful, I worked my last ninety days at my old practice and signed the lease for a 2,500 square feet office with six exam rooms. I started to learn how to develop protocols and search for staff. I acquired a loan of $200,000 (with personal guarantee) to renovate the office, as well as cover supplies and initial salaries.

During my two months off period, I established a phone line and a basic website for patients to find me. I personally answered calls and scheduled patients. To my greatest surprise, my patients were looking for me! Five months after my resignation, my practice, Alta Vista Dermatology, opened with twenty patients on the first day!

I worked with one full- and two part-time, cross-trained employees, five days a week. We grew in small increments, and some days it felt like two steps back instead of forward. But ultimately, each year we have grown.

I attribute this growth to a strong mission-based vision to help create healthy skin that boosts self-confidence and influences lives. Over long days, purpose-driven hard work and steadfast faith lead me and my team.

Our goal has been to establish a strong, supportive *team* in the office (which is crucial), a team that always focuses on providing outstanding clinical care and customer service. We made our fair share of small and big mistakes, like with our first EMR and billing company, but we embrace the roller coaster of ups and downs. Celebrating successes and persevering after failures, as I've learned, are the secrets of champions.

So what helped us to thrive when most businesses fail within the first few years of their existence? I hired our first provider, a nurse practitioner, five months after opening the practice, along with an aesthetician. Slowly added providers, more front and back office, and a manager. Although we have been conservative with finances, expansion of staff, space, and technology, we have developed a state-of-the-art facility to serve our community. This allowed us a steady growth to a multi-seven-figure-revenue business with three physicians, five physician assistants, three aestheticians, and a staff of thirty-eight.

Most importantly, I finally feel that I am serving, helping, and making a difference the way I want to. By impacting the skin health and glow of many, I can live my most authentic life. Choosing impact is more difficult than being a follower but essential for a fulfilling life.

Impact is possible—I am a living proof. Get started!

Author: Dr. Sarolta K. Szabo

Dr. Sarolta Szabo is a board-certified, fellowship-trained dermatologist and is a past president of the Colorado Dermatologic Society. She is the founder, medical director, and CEO of Alta Vista Dermatology in Highlands Ranch, Colorado. A comprehensive dermatology practice that has offered general, surgical, and aesthetic services since 2010, Alta Vista Dermatology is dedicated to excelling in creating healthy, glowing skin that empowers self-confidence.

Dr. Szabo is a top doctor, author, speaker, wife, mom of four boys, and outdoor enthusiast who enjoys integrating mindfulness and nutrition to create a natural balance in the skin and environment. You can follow her on Instagram: @drszaboderm.

CHAPTER 43

EMBRACING
ENTREPRENEURSHIP

S oon after completing my ophthalmology residency, I found myself in a solo practice with no business skills. My training had prepared me with a wonderful set of clinical and surgical skills, but I found out that I was not prepared for the world of running a business.

Working for myself has always been a dream of mine. I loved the idea of having control over my own time and the limitless earning potential one can achieve, so I went into a solo practice with great enthusiasm. However, I never believed that I was an entrepreneur; I thought that I was just a physician who happened to own a practice. Over time, my lack of the business and management skills needed to run a business led to significant self-doubt that impacted all aspects of my practice.

I made many mistakes along the way that kept the practice from growing. I did not have a clear vision and focus for the practice, and as a result, I poorly communicated my needs and goals to my staff. This led to a lot of frustration. I made mistakes in hiring and in setting up systems for clinic efficiency. I even let fear keep me from promoting the practice and relied solely on word of mouth. I leaned on what I knew I was good at, which was the clinical aspect, and thought that everything else would just fall into place. But it did not.

Furthermore, I did not fully appreciate the value of the surgical and clinical expertise I brought to the patients I served. My patients would tell me how much their vision and lives had changed as a result of working with me, but because I did not equate pricing to the value of the services that I offered, I completely avoided pricing. Ultimately, the practice suffered. I was giving out great value but getting little in return. Through the years, I developed feelings of burnout, isolation, and anxiety. I was working hard but not bringing in the revenue that I believed I should at that point of my career.

Not only had the feelings of inadequacy and fear kept my practice from growing, but they also showed up in my personal life. I was constantly anxious, feeling like I was not providing for my family. I even considered selling the practice many times. I felt that when it came to managing and running the business side of the practice, someone else would surely be better at it than me. However, something inside just would not let me do it. I had put so much into the practice—sweat, tears, and even our savings.

The turning point for me was the COVID-19 pandemic when everything shut down, including my practice that was already struggling. While spending more time at home with my family, I started thinking of ways to bring in other streams of revenue to supplement my income.

I always had a love for real estate and decided to take a course in real estate investing. I was attending a virtual real estate conference for physicians, and I happened to hear a speaker say that she helps physicians build profitable businesses. The idea of helping physicians practice medicine on their own terms was very inspirational to me. I had never encountered anyone or any program that helped physicians succeed in business.

Her name was Dr. Nneka Unachukwu (Dr. Una), and that was her mission. I found out that she created the EntreMD Business School with the sole purpose of helping physicians have successful businesses. At that moment, my mind completely left real estate and went directly to my struggling practice, and I thought that this could be the answer to getting myself and my practice unstuck.

Enrolling in the business school was one of the best decisions that I have made for myself and my practice. I have come to realize that I have been an entrepreneur all along.

I guided and managed my practice through a pandemic and continued to provide patients with great services and quality eye care. The tools that I have received from the business school allowed me to gain a clearer vision for the practice, and I am able to communicate it with my staff. We have streamlined processes to better our patients' experience, and wait time has decreased by 50 percent. Our collections are up, and revenue has increased by 30 percent. We now have a more solid social media presence and advertising on local platforms, and these avenues have helped to bring new patients into the practice. All these changes have occurred within a matter of months of gaining the knowledge, skills, and tools to improve my business.

Furthermore, my confidence has grown by leaps and bounds. I now understand my value and expertise in a whole new light. I have a deeper appreciation of the impact my skills have on my patients as well as the community and society. This has allowed me to clearly communicate what I offer.

I no longer let fear keep me back. I feel more present and truly feel that I am walking in my purpose.

Now I completely embrace being called an entrepreneur. It took a while, but my mindset has shifted. Having the resources and guidance from a community of other physician entrepreneurs, I will continue to strive to reach my greatest potential. I look forward to a brighter, more fulfilled future for myself and my business.

Author: Dr. Carola B. Okogbaa

Dr. Carola Okogbaa is a board-certified ophthalmologist serving in Baton Rouge, Louisiana since 2013. She specializes in the medical and surgical treatment of eye diseases and is the CEO and founder of Louisiana Center for Eyes, a comprehensive eye clinic that helps individuals achieve their best vision.

Dr. Okogbaa loves to spend time with her husband of twenty-two years and their three children. You can follow her on Facebook: @lacenterforeyes.

CHAPTER 44

ON BEING **AFRAID** AND DOING IT ANYWAY

Fear is my greatest friend and my worst enemy. It can motivate me or paralyze me. With that awareness, I keep my friends close and my enemy closer.

Knowing the enemy well allows me to control it before it controls me and leaves me stagnant, but maintaining a mindset to keep the enemy under control requires various weapons. Many I have successfully wielded thus far. However, new weapons will need to be acquired and honed along my journey as I rejoin with fear as my friend, ever progressing through the complexities of being a physician in today's world.

I remember the day I decided I was done with corporate medicine. I had returned from maternity leave after a complicated pregnancy and was told they were doing away with my evening patient hours. "What? Say that again." I couldn't believe my ears.

For a year, I had petitioned and had finally gotten my evening office hours approved. On the late days, patients and their families wouldn't miss school or work to see me. Those late days also allowed me to leave an hour earlier the other days of the week so that I could be home and present for my kids, attempting to practice what I preach as a child and adolescent psychiatrist. It worked great for over a year, but during my leave, the higher-ups reversed it.

What now? A newborn, less time home with my kids, and a feeling of increasing disregard for the needs of myself and my patients. Weekend calls had already gone from four-hour rounding days to twelve hours without additional compensation. The balance had shifted, and I was done.

I went home that night and shared the news with my husband. We agreed, enough is enough. It was time for me to consider opening my own practice.

Throughout residency and fellowship, when I was dreaming/ planning/training, friendly fear motivated me to ask as many questions as I could. "Could I get copies of your intake forms, your note templates, and questionnaires?" Whereas a majority of my peers focused solely on the clinical supervision piece, I went beyond just clinical. I would ask about rent and liability, malpractice, and reimbursements. How they billed. How they decided what to charge. How they handled delinquent payments. How they screened new potential patients. Did they have any fears or regrets?

There was no course for these things during my training, and I wanted to know it all back then. I kept files of the various practice styles and forms in folders. I packed them in the moving truck with the rest of my cherished belongings when we moved to my first post-fellowship job. For someday...

After my evening hours were cut, I enrolled in a few courses on how to run a business, one from the local community college and another from a mentor in my field. I had always imagined owning my own practice someday, just not then (fear, the enemy, kept it at a distance). But over the next few days, I pulled out those folders, reviewed my notes, culled the forms for the data, and created my own forms. I compiled others' work in a style I could call my own. The busy work during those days was a distraction from the fear I had of leaving a salaried job and entering the uncharted.

I had no clue how to resign, so I called a lawyer friend, and she referred me to a contract lawyer. He helped me with the resignation letter and confirmed that I would not violate a noncompete if I opened ten miles outside the clinic radius.

Over the next several weeks, I asked more questions of my accountant, colleagues, mentors, psychiatric societies, and family. I was petrified. Would my patients follow? Could they? Where would I practice? Could I do this without a support staff? Could I afford support staff?

After a few sleepless nights, I called my neighbor, a stay-at-home mom whose kids were in school and who hopefully had some time to help. She was the most organized person I knew. The type that sets out bowls, spoons, and cereal boxes the night before so mornings worked like a clock. Always on time, everything where it needed to be. Just what I needed.

She said yes, so together we started looking for rentals. She is with me to this day.

I negotiated with the clinic to send letters to my patients that I was leaving and opening a fee-for-service private practice, with a number to reach me if interested in following me. The charts and client list belonged to the hospital. The patients belonged to themselves.

Fear asked, *Who was going to go from insured to self-pay?* Amazingly, over 40 percent followed from day one. Referrals from therapists and doctors I'd worked with poured in. Eventually, another 20–30 percent joined me. Within three months, I started a waitlist for new patients. I was humbled. Eleven years in, and my practice remains full with new patients joining as old patients move or happily no longer need my services.

Patient care carries a toll. Boundaries prevent me from increasing hours, so I recently diversified my finite energy. With my fear friend/foe buzzing around me, I ventured into my latest endeavor—creating a safe space for women professionals to navigate stress through meaningful connections, explorations in play, presence, and self-care.

Applying my skills and knowledge in this forum has been self-preservational. However, having never had to market my practice, yet needing to do so for this venture, has created challenges. Once again, the battle between paralyzing and motivational fear rages. New weapons are wielded. Through collaboration with like-minded entrepreneurs and the ever-asking mindset, I am defeating the enemy form of fear and pushing through to a successful, meaningful, and joyful adventure.

Success has many meanings; for me, it is feeling purpose, joy, balance, and grace, even at times when I feel afraid…and doing it anyway.

Author: Dr. Randie Schacter, DO, DFAACAP

Randie Schacter, DO, DFAACAP, is the founder/owner of Silver Psychiatric Services.

She is the past president of the Charlotte Area Psychiatric Society, the North Carolina Council of Child and Adolescent Psychiatry's current delegate to the AACAP Assembly, coeditor to their newsletter, and speaks professionally on gender differences in burnout.

Dr. Schacter is the creator/owner of an interactive CME program for Women Medical Professionals, reducing stress and burnout with meditation and art, accompanied by farm-to-table meals. Smiles, data, and testimonials tell it best.

She lives in Matthews, North Carolina with her husband and three daughters. Follow her on Instagram: @silver.spaces.

CHAPTER 45

CHANGE YOUR MINDSET, CHANGE YOUR **REALITY**

I knew going into radiation oncology was going to be the best career decision when I graduated from medical school. I knew medicine was my calling, and I was so excited to be given the chance to try to cure and help people who had been diagnosed with cancer.

Owning my own practice was something that I had always dreamed about, but for most of the seventeen years I have been practicing radiation oncology, I have worked for other people. However, in 2019, I decided to start my own practice, providing professional radiation oncology services to a radiation oncology clinic that was already in existence. This meant leasing office space and leasing all of the radiation equipment from a management company who would also provide some management oversight. I signed a ten-year lease, and I opened my doors in September 2019.

Then one day in March 2020, right at the start of the COVID-19 pandemic, I received a call from the management company. They informed me that they had decided to reorganize their business, and that meant they were closing the office in two months. I would have to shut my medical practice down and vacate, or I could buy the facility from them and all of the equipment as well.

I was in shock, and I could feel the fear start to overcome all of my thoughts. I had just started my practice a few months earlier. I was still learning how to be a solo practitioner in private practice, and I wasn't ready to buy the entire facility and all of the equipment. I also knew leaving and going back to an employed position was going to be extremely difficult, given the very tight job market in radiation oncology. All I could focus on was if I did not have a job anymore, how would I keep my kids in their schools? How would I pay my bills? How would I stay in the house where I was living?

That was truly a make-or-break moment for me, and I was scared. The negative thoughts and doubts kept coming, and I struggled with the overwhelming feeling of taking all of this on in just two months.

I had never done any of this before, but I had always wanted to eventually own my own practice and radiation oncology equipment. Additionally, I knew that the most important thing was for me to be able to provide for my family. I could not let fear make any decisions for me.

So I changed my mindset and embraced the challenge—I decided to buy the clinic and all of the equipment. I was going to finally be in full control of my career, and I was excited at the thought of becoming an entrepreneur.

Fall came, and things were going great. By September, I had purchased the equipment, hired employees, and negotiated a new long-term lease with the building landlord, all while in the middle of the pandemic. The physicians who had been referring to me when I first opened in 2019 continued to refer, and I was seeing a lot of patients. I brought my husband on to be my practice manager and hired a physician liaison to do my marketing, which was instrumental in gaining new referrals from other physicians. I got a website designed and launched and developed marketing materials with branded products. I also initiated an email marketing campaign targeted to my referring physicians to keep them up to date about cancer topics and news about my practice.

I knew I would need to put myself out there more, so I began focusing on networking. I joined two different mastermind groups and began researching entrepreneurship topics on the internet. I found the EntreMD Business School website and joined to learn how to be a better physician entrepreneur. I focused on increasing my social media following and joined a mom's entrepreneur club. My enjoyment of working with my patients led me to start a podcast about cancer so I could bring guests on the show and we could discuss topics that were important to people touched by cancer. This year, I was awarded *Los Angeles Magazine*'s Top Doctor award in radiation oncology for the fifth year in a row.

The management company's decision to move their business in a different direction gave me the opportunity to push myself into entrepreneurship. It forced me to confront my fears and limiting beliefs about myself and my capabilities. I changed my mindset and started thinking and acting like a business owner. I embraced the idea of taking a huge risk, and I saw the challenges that would no doubt be ahead of me as an opportunity for growth.

I am so proud of everything I have accomplished, and I am also proud of the internal work I have done to build my confidence to take action. The practice is now very successful; I am continuing to see growth in the number of patient referrals for radiation therapy. I have a great staff who really cares about the patients, and we are doing great work.

Personally, I have grown in ways that I never envisioned. Entrepreneurship and owning my own practice has definitely not been easy. It has been stressful and at times very discouraging, but working on my mindset has kept me focused on the goals and tasks.

Every day there are challenges, obstacles, and uncertainties that I face, but this process has reaffirmed the importance of understanding that you are enough. Constantly working on your mindset, and not letting fearful and negative thoughts guide your actions, can lead you to a life you always dreamed of having.

Author: Dr. Rosalyn Morrell

Dr. Rosalyn Morrell is a board-certified radiation oncologist and founder and CEO of CenterPoint Radiation Oncology. She utilizes her extensive expertise in using the most advanced therapies to treat all types of cancer with radiation therapy. She has been a guest on various podcasts and radio shows, has her own podcast for cancer patients called *Cancer from A to Z*, and is a frequent speaker on cancer treatment and health disparities.

Dr. Morrell lives in Los Angeles with her husband and two kids. You can follow her on Instagram: @dr_rosalynmorrell.

CHAPTER 46

MY **BONUS** LIFE

A s I look back at my life, it seems that new beginnings have been a familiar theme. In the summer of 1979, my parents left Iran on a two-week planned vacation, which coincided with the start of the Iranian Revolution and the yearlong American embassy hostage crisis. Having packed only a suitcase each, we ended up setting roots for a permanent life in the United States.

My parents were not entrepreneurs, but their philosophy was "work hard, become educated, and you will succeed." Higher education had always been at the top of their list. My father was never able to work as a civil engineer in the United States, but he attempted to start several small businesses without success.

That was my limited experience of entrepreneurial life, and I decided that one has to be born business-savvy and have the special genes to be successful in business. That is why after finishing residency, being an employed physician was the only option that I ever considered. *I could never own a business or run my own practice*, I thought.

All of these limiting beliefs were extensively tested when, at the age of forty-four, I was diagnosed with ovarian cancer, and I had time to review my personal and professional life. I knew the dismal statistics for survival, and I had already begun to grieve missing out on my kids' middle school, high school, and college graduation ceremonies. As I spent time reexamining my life, recurring questions kept invading my thoughts: *Have I fulfilled my potential?*

I realized that my identity was so interlaced with being an eye surgeon that with the looming possibility of chemo-induced neuropathy, I had to reevaluate who I would be if I could no longer be an ophthalmologist. How would I live a life of purpose? Surely, I was not *done*. I decided to focus on my faith and live my life one day, one chemo session, and sometimes one hour at a time.

By 2019, I had passed my five-year survival mark and considered myself a warrior. I knew there would continue to be times in my life when I would have doubts and feel paralyzed with indecision, but I did not want to look back on my life with regret. To celebrate my "bonus life," I tattooed the Farsi word for "warrior" on my left wrist as a reminder of my strengths, perseverance, and motivation.

With this new mindset, I returned from an eight-month medical leave to my employed position. I became aware of a deeper connection with my patients, and I felt fulfilled when advocating for them. I had begun to find my voice. However, I did not have any power or control over the major decisions regarding the practice. That is when I formally expressed my desire to become a partner.

They denied my request without an adequate reason. I knew that if I stayed, nothing would change, and I was no longer content.

This solidified my decision to leave the security of my employed ophthalmology position, with its steady paycheck, after thirteen years. I closed that door right at the beginning of the COVID-19 pandemic and made a leap of faith by opening another. I was scared, but I was certain about my loyal patient following. I knew that they *needed* someone like me.

It is unbelievable how the universe helps open doors just when you feel trapped. I began sharing space with a reputable optometry practice known for incredible patient care. About the time I knew that I needed to learn about scaling my private practice, I discovered *The EntreMD Podcast*. It was an excellent start, but I needed more. So I took a step further and invested in my personal and professional growth by joining the EntreMD Business School (EBS).

Soon after starting the course, I realized that I was not alone. I was among like-minded visionaries who wanted more than to just practice traditional medicine. Most of these physicians knew that their potential was limitless. I wanted to believe that I would come to the same realization that my potential is limitless and that I am responsible for my success.

EBS emphasizes challenges to grow your brand, your business, and your practice. I watched as my colleagues participated in doing Facebook live videos on various topics. I kept thinking they were so brave to speak up and post regularly and that I could never do that. I watched and listened while others participated in the challenges. I noticed that the ones who participated had more "wins" to report.

With each subsequent challenge, I practiced putting myself out there. At first, I was struggling to go on social media and share my voice. Nothing felt comfortable. I cannot tell you how many times I rehearsed my introduction video on my morning commute to work. As soon as I parked the car, I would tell myself, "No, today is not a good day."

Finally, with the encouragement of my EBS sisters, I made a video announcing that I would go live on Facebook every Monday at 8:00 a.m. Yet another door had been opened, and there was no turning back. I was nervous, uncomfortable, and scared, but that Monday, I successfully delivered my first live video. I felt relief and pride. I realized I did not need to be born with business genes; I simply had to lean into my community and take action.

This journey into entrepreneurship has been one of self-discovery. As part of building our brands, we were challenged to go on podcasts. What would I say and who would want to hear my story? My first interview on Dr. Tamara Beckford's podcast was transformed into part of a four-day virtual cancer summit. Sharing my story was a reminder of my strengths and appreciation for my transformation during my life journey.

Since opening my ophthalmology private practice, I have reached a much wider audience and become more comfortable with connecting on social media. Since joining EBS, I have matched my employed production numbers. However, the most dramatic change has been one of mindset. I have converted from the idea that one must be born to succeed in business to knowing that I will learn all about growing my brand and knowing that my practice will thrive when I take massive action.

I want you to live this life as if it *is* your bonus life. You are not too old, and it is not too late. Learn these lessons from people like me so that you don't have to go through a traumatic event to appreciate the opportunities you have at hand.

First, be honest with what you envision for your personal and professional life. Then invest time and money in the network that can help you achieve it 1,000 times faster than doing it alone.

It has been only six months since I joined EBS, and I am already looking back at the person I used to be, proud of all that I have accomplished, and looking forward to all the milestones I have yet to achieve. Be daring now and pursue the life you've dreamed of.

Author: Dr. Mitra Ayazifar

Dr. Mitra Ayazifar is an eye surgeon in private practice living in Northern California. She specializes in cataract surgery, along with cosmetic and functional lid procedures.

As the CEO of Capital Eye Medical Group, she partners with patients to develop their best potential vision so that they can live life fully and enjoy their hobbies for years to come. She believes that she treats more than her patients' eyes.

Dr. Mitra is also an ovarian cancer survivor who continues to share her journey while living her "bonus life." She lives near Sacramento with her family. Follow her adventures on Instagram: @mitramd3.

CHAPTER 47

RUN YOUR **OWN** RACE

In the Marathon and in Your Business

F ive years into my job as a pediatric hospitalist, I wanted to
quit medicine. I was so very tired. The flipping of schedules
from day shift to night shift and back again, the staying late long
after my shift was over to sign out patients to my colleagues and to
complete charting, and all of those holidays away from my family
and missed special occasions because of work began to take a
toll. On my days off from the hospital, I would look at the calendar and be filled with a sense of dread when I saw the night shift
coming up.

Standing in the back of the emergency department during
a shift one night, watching the staff scurry about, I thought to
myself, *Why are you here if you dread coming here?* I wanted out. I
wanted more. I wanted to step off this treadmill. In the back of that

emergency department, questioning my major life decisions up to that point, I decided to sign up for my first marathon.

Perhaps training for a marathon during a time of major burnout in my clinical role doesn't seem like the next logical step, but I assure you, it changed everything. Preparing to run that distance requires spending a lot of time with oneself on the pavement, which is one of the reasons I fell in love with running in the first place.

Now, I wasn't always a runner. When I was a kid, I huffed and puffed my way around the track, frequently walking to complete a workout. I used to think the cross-country team had a different genetic makeup than I did.

After my wonderful dad passed away in November 2012, however, I started regularly lacing up my sneakers and taking myself around the block, five or ten minutes at a time. I found that I loved the peace I experienced out on the run. All the thoughts in my head grew quiet and I could just focus on my footfalls—one foot in front of the other. It was during the long runs in preparation for this race that I began to work through the grief and loss I had experienced five years earlier.

The marathon was a transformative experience for me. When I returned home after the race, I wanted to shout from the rooftops that everyone should go out and run 26.2 miles as soon as possible. In particular, I became passionate about telling everyone I knew that they should start running and that it would change their lives!

I began writing training plans to help friends and family get started with running. I talked about running to all who would listen. I made the decision to get my run coach certification with the Road Runners Club of America (RRCA). Passion met purpose when I started my run coach business, Mindful Marathon, in 2019.

Since then, I've helped hundreds of runners get started with running as well as run their first ever 5K races, half marathons, and marathons. I've coached runners to pursue new race distances and personal bests that they never thought possible.

I'm an introvert, and I've done so many things outside my comfort zone in just two short years: started a blog, started a YouTube channel, became a guest on over twenty podcasts, wrote pieces for magazines, landed paid speaking gigs, and had the opportunity to collaborate with so many amazing and inspiring runners, physicians, and experts in fitness and wellness. In fall of 2021, I became a race director and put on a sold-out virtual 5K for one hundred runners! I am on a mission to make running more approachable and more doable, to show that it doesn't have to be so hard and can be enjoyable.

Much like running, entrepreneurship doesn't have to be so hard either. You may be thinking, *I'm a full-time clinician. I don't have time to build a business, and I don't know where to start.* There is a simple way. We start by starting.

In running, we train from a place of current fitness, whether that means we are coming from the couch or coming to the sport from a more experienced place. The same is true in business. It is okay to start where you are and to grow at your own pace. As physicians, it can be difficult to put blinders on and not compare ourselves to where others are in their businesses. But we have to remember, everyone is running their own race. Embrace yours.

There are a lot of burned-out physicians right now, but there is hope. We have it within ourselves to change the narrative. I am both a pediatrician *and* a run coach, and the roles complement each other. Looking back, I don't think it's any surprise that Mindful Marathon grew out of that time of burnout and that time of introspection during marathon training. The time spent running helped me to tap into who I am and into who I want to be.

The runner who registers for that first marathon and lines up at the start line is not the same runner who crosses the marathon finish line. This is one of the many reasons why I love the marathon so much, and why I love to coach runners to this distance.

I learned and am still learning to fall in love with the process: in running and in my business. It's not just about the finish line of the race or about the shiny medal that we get to hang on the wall as evidence. It's about the transformation that takes place along the way. It's about who we become in the process.

Author: Dr. Michelle Quirk

Dr. Michelle Quirk is a primary care pediatrician and RRCA-certified run coach. She is the founder and CEO of Mindful Marathon, where she helps make running easy and fun for busy professionals. She is the host of *Mindful Marathon Conversations* on YouTube, where she has interviewed many inspiring runners and athletes including ultrarunner Charlie Engle. Finally, Dr. Quirk has served as a guest on multiple podcasts and led a mindful movement run/walk session at the ACE Conference for Women Physicians.

She lives in Philadelphia, Pennsylvania with her husband, Tony. You can follow her on Instagram: @mindful.marathon.

SECTION III AUTHORS

Dr. Nikki Gorman

Dr. Rose Marie Thomas

Dr. Elizabeth Chiang, PhD

Dr. Rashmi Schramm

Dr. Minako Abe

Dr. Amelia L. Bueche

Dr. Catherine H. Toomer

Dr. Carola B. Okogbaa

Dr. Sarolta K. Szabo

Dr. Randie Schacter

Dr. Rosalyn Morrell

Dr. Michelle Quirk

Dr. Mitra Ayazifar

CONCLUSION

There you have it! Over forty stories of physicians just like you who are growing or scaling their businesses. As the editor of this book, I have had the privilege of reading these stories over and over again.

It is important for us as physicians to realize that we have very brilliant business ideas. If it doesn't seem that way, you've now learned how to take inventory of the possible profitable business ideas you already have. Once you take inventory, it is time to launch and grow your business. You may have been told it is not possible, but you have just read the stories of so many doctors who have done just that.

To me, this is evidence that *this is the best of times for physicians.*

Today, I want to invite you to start or take the next step in your journey, and there are three things you can do.

Commit to doing one thing to start or grow your business. As you read this book, you probably came across a story that highlighted the next step for you. Don't wait; get it done.

If you haven't started your business, your next step could be to choose a name and register your LLC. If you already own a business but you're struggling to get patients or clients, now is a great time to decide to put yourself out there. It may look like reaching out to referral sources, asking to be a guest on podcasts, or simply sending out an email to your list inviting people to work with you.

Stay inspired. Inspiration wears off, and that is why I have developed that habit of setting myself up to be inspired every single day. I do this by listening to podcasts, reading books, and surrounding myself with successful entrepreneurs, either on social media or in person.

I recommend you subscribe to *The EntreMD Podcast.* You will get access to episodes that will keep you motivated and in action. Think about it like a pocket MBA just for doctors. Also, if there were any stories that really resonated with you, follow the author on social media and check out their work.

Find your tribe. You've heard it before: you are the average of the five people you spend the most time with. The right people will normalize the challenges you will face as an entrepreneur, consistently serve as a source of inspiration, and hold you accountable. If you want to be in a community of physicians just like the ones you just read about, you can. Come join us in the EntreMD Business School.

As an introvert, I can understand if anyone feels intimidated by this, but the right relationship will fast-track your journey as an entrepreneur. What if you had five firebrand entrepreneurs in your circle? You would become the sixth! Don't skip this.

I have so much faith in you and the business idea you have. Don't hold back, go all-in, because this is our time.

I am rooting for you, and I can't wait to celebrate all your successes.

—Dr. Una

ABOUT THE AUTHOR

DR. NNEKA UNACHUKWU is a board-certified pediatrician and the founder and CEO of Ivy League Pediatrics outside of Atlanta, Georgia. She graduated from the University of Nigeria College of Medicine and completed her residency in New Jersey before opening her own practice.

Fondly known as Dr. Una, she founded EntreMD in response to drastic shifts for doctors in the healthcare field, including loss of autonomy, job insecurity, and unparalleled dissatisfaction. The mission of EntreMD is to help doctors build profitable businesses so they can live life and practice medicine on their own terms. Her popular offerings include the EntreMD Business School, live events, The EntreMD Podcast, and the bestselling EntreMD Method book. The podcast is listened to in over one hundred countries and has exceeded 280,000 downloads in two years. She is a highly sought-after speaker, a regular contributor to Forbes, and a member of the Forbes Business Council.

Dr. Una and her husband, Steve, have been married for sixteen years and are the proud parents of four children—Cheta, Chidi, Chichi, and Esther. They live near Atlanta, Georgia.

Made in the USA
Las Vegas, NV
26 January 2023

66278932R00185